I0466859

Debt And Equity Financing Strategies For Your Company

SADANAND PUJARI

Published by SADANAND PUJARI, 2024.

Table of Contents

Copyright

Debt And Equity Financing Strategies For Your Company

First Edition: Jun 2024

Book Design by **SADANAND PUJARI**

About

In this Book you learn about the financing strategies for your business throughout its lifecycle. You also learn about all the major debt and equity financing arrangements at an application based level.

In the debt section of the Book, you learn about how operating lines of credit work and what to watch out for. We also talk about asset based lending facilities, term loans, and leasing. Mezzanine financing is an increasingly popular way of replacing equity financing with hybrid financial instruments.

In the equity section of the Book, you learn about venture capital, private equity, and the process of going public. Finally, you learn about how the cost of capital and capital structure factor into your strategic thinking and decision making.

Introduction

We want to basically make investments so that we can get a return on the investments. When you're thinking of investments, you might be thinking about long term types of project investments. You might be thinking about investing in fixed assets that will hopefully help us to generate a return.

The goal of the investments, Of course, is for the future return. So the idea typically for most businesses is that we need some money, the funding in order to invest so that we can then get a return. Hopefully that return is better than the cost of the financing in order to invest. Note, as you're thinking about these concepts, you might be in a type of business or think of some type of industries where there aren't a lot of costs to basically start up. And that might be the case. But typically in those types of areas, there's also more competition involved. Oftentimes there's going to be investments that need to be made in some way, shape or form, money that needs to be invested for projects for the capital.

And then obviously, how are we going to get the funds in order to invest and then get the return on them? So then the funds are going to be needed for the investments. So now we need the funds for the investments. The financing options include debt financing and equity financing. So now we're thinking, OK, well, how are we going to get the funds? There's two kinds of broad categories that we can do. We could take debt financing at which time we borrow the money in some way, shape or form. We're going to owe back that money plus interest on it.

We're basically renting the money, the interest we can think of as the rent on the money.

And we're going to pay back the principal as well, just like if we had an apartment or something like that or an office space. We have to pay for the office space and then we have to give back the office space at the end in the same kind of concept. But when we have this type of financing, the interest is also often deductible for taxes. So we have a tax impact on the equity side of things we could think about. Well, why don't we basically issue stock if we're a corporation providing an equity interest in the corporation, given a piece of in essence, kind of the value the corporation retained earnings in the future, growth potential in the organization as well.

Also, as you do that, however, then if you're giving retained earnings, you're also having the voting rights and so on being involved with that type of financing option. So that's what you're going to do. Those are your options to get the funds that are going to be needed. So that's the basic scenario. Then, Of course, we have and we're thinking about the financing options. We got investments that we need to make for some future type of return. We need the funds in order to have the investments. And then our options are going to be debt financing and equity financing. Then, Of course, our questions are, well, what kind of financing is available to us? What kind of rates are available to us for the cost of that financing and what would be our optimal mix of financing options so that we can basically choose the best option for the financing.

So earnings generally need to be greater than the fund acquisition costs, the costs of financing. So obviously when we're thinking about taking on some kind of cost of financing, either by taking on some type of debt or by some equity financing in order to invest in some way in equipment plants or whatnot, then Of course, our goal is to say, well, is our expected return. We only want to do this if our expected return is greater than the cost of financing in general. So the cost of the capital decision making process.

So now we're thinking about the cost of the capital, what's going to be the decision making process in order to decide what projects we might do or what type of financing options we might have. The decision to invest in something should not be based on specific financing options. And this is when it gets a little bit confusing, because when we think about certain types of investments, we think about the financing that's going to be connected to that particular investment. But we also want to think about it basically in the context of our capital structure, our financing structure basically as a whole in general, what we would like to have is some type of rape.

Basically, it's going to be our minimum rate or our required rate of return that we can apply to the projects that would be independent to some degree of the financing options so that we can then think about it in terms of this minimum rate of return, so that we can then be comparing different projects possibly that have similar or possibly different financing options and make decisions in that way. If we were to do so, if we were to make our decision specific to the financing options, we could have inconsistent investment decisions. So if we narrow our focus to a particular financing option, instead of taking a broader view, we might make less than optimal decisions.

Financing decisions should be made with an understanding of the company's capital structure, so that's going to be the general rule, the general idea that you want to basically have in your mind. We have the financing that we're going to be taking in place so that we can make our investments. We have the breakout between the options, typically have debt financing, equity financing, and we would like to make our decisions in some format with taking into consideration the weighting of the capital structure. And we'll talk more about how to do that in future chapters.

Weighted Average Cost of Capital WACC

Remember, we're thinking about financing options, major to financing options of the operations of the organization of the company being debt financing, equity financing. So we'll go through this formula in total and then we'll think about in future chapters and with practice problems how to calculate certain components of this formula that you can then put into perspective within the formula. So remember, as we think about our financing options, we want to get an idea of our capital structure. This is one way to do so.

So we've got the task equals E over D plus E times R E plus D over E plus E times R D times one minus T, where E is the market value of equity d the market value of debt or E is the cost of equity in R, D is the cost of debt. And then the tax is going to be the tax amount for T. Now this looks very intimidating and confusing. We'll break down these two components here D over D plus E and D over D plus E shortly. And then these two items are E and R of D are basically the cost of debt and the cost of equity. And you can think about the cost of debt, probably the more straightforward one for people to think about. If you're issuing something like bonds, which we'll talk about in the future, then you have a situation where you're going to be paying, Of course, the interest on the bonds.

We issue bonds in order to generate revenue, in order to get funds for the financing, we're going to have to pay for it with interest. That's going to be the rent on it. And there's going to be a tax impact, which is going to be something that we're going to be thinking about for the debt. That's one of the things that makes it confusing when we consider debt financing and equity financing, because we have that tax impact on the equity side of things, we're typically thinking the common type of thing to issue being common stock, which means we're giving ownership in essence to the company, giving in essence, value of the retained earnings assets minus liabilities, the equity value of the company.

That one is also confusing to calculate here, more confusing than basically the interest in concept, because we have to basically make assumptions about the future. What's the value of the company? What's going to be the growth of the company? So these two concepts, we will then go into future chapters and and think about how to calculate them more as we go these to the division items here over D plus E and over plus E, we're going to think about conceptually here and we won't do a lot of problems on this component or in this chapter because we're going to be focusing in on our practice problems to calculate these two items. So let's break this down a little bit further.

Let's first start with our accounting equations or our accounting equation is assets, equal liabilities plus equity. Equity assets are what the company has liabilities and equity are who has claim in essence to those assets. So whatever the company has, then third parties liabilities have claims to them outside of the organization. Equity represents the owner. And if we're talking about a corporation, we're talking about stockholders equity. So these two liabilities and equity we could think of as financing the assets, the assets will then be used in order to generate the revenue. Now, you can kind of think about this on a book basis or a market basis, and that gets a little bit kind of confusing because, you know, the accounting, the accounting versus the fair market versus the market value and whatnot.

But just conceptually, we have here the accounting equation assets, equal liabilities plus equity liabilities and equity and the financing options. If we rewrite the accounting equation, we could see assets equal and we're just going to say debt now instead of liabilities. We're just going to call it debt plus equity assets, equal debt plus equity, because that's the terminology we're going to be using in our formulas from a financing perspective. And then we can use our algebra here to solve for equity, which would give us equity equals assets minus debt. So equity within equals the assets minus the debt.

And that's a useful way to see the formula, because that shows us that the equity, which in this case stockholders equity we're talking about a corporation, is basically the value of of the organization, meaning assets of the organization, what they have, minus the debt, the liabilities, what's owed to third parties is the value of the organization. So when you think about equity financing, issuing common stocks, in essence for a corporation, you're kind of thinking about this as a useful way to think about the accounting equation. So then we can look at the debt percent. If we look at the debt percent, that would be the debt over the assets. So we have our calculation here.

We can think of the debt over the assets and the equity over the assets. And the sum of those two should be one hundred percent. This is going to be our weight that we will have so much debt over the assets. Notice that the assets down here, we show that assets are equal to debt plus equity. So assets are equal to debt plus equity. So I can write this as debt over debt plus equity debt over assets is equivalent to saying debt over debt plus equity because debt plus equity is equivalent to the assets. And then over here we can say the equity percent. If we think about the equity percent, it would be equity over assets.

Simply rewriting our equation here or thinking about our equation in terms of debt over assets and then equity over assets, the two of those then have to equal then one hundred percent and we have equity over assets is the equivalent to saying equity over debt plus equity, because once again, debt plus equity is assets, assets, equal debt plus equity. So these are the two kinds of components, the ratio components of our formula. We won't spend a lot of time on calculating those in our practice problems, but you can get an idea for it conceptually here. So if we go back to our formula, that in essence is going to be this item and this item. So we won't spend a lot of time on those two, we're going to be spending our time on R, E and R d the cost of debt and the cost of equity.

So that's going to be our calculations. So we looked at these two basically conceptually as waiting between debt and equity. And then we consider basically our cost of debt and cost of equity with relation to it. And then these to the cost of debt and equity are going to be somewhat complicated to calculate. And that's what we'll focus on in our time, remembering that the cost of debt will have taken into consideration the tax impact. Now, you can write this down and basically like a table format down below. So you can basically put this format, this formula into like a table down here for something like this would look something like this. We will work on a practice problem with this. So I highly recommend working through the practice problems.

We have the debt. So if the cost of debt and this debt is after taxes, it's already taken into consideration the tax impact up top is six percent. So that would mean that if we think about that cost of debt, we're saying this is the financing cost for us, financing costs for debt typically being interest. But when we think about interest and we want to weigh it against other financing costs, such as equity financing, we want to take into account the cost of the taxes or the impact of the taxes, which are actually a tax benefit. So when we think about the interest rate, we'll have to adjust it. When we think about bonds, which is one of the most confusing ones to do in this category, we would say, OK, the interest rate is what it is, the rate on the bond or the market rate? Typically, we'll use the market rate.

We'll get into more detail on that, why we would do that. And then and then we have to think, well, now there's a tax impact for it as well. What's going to be the tax impact so we can see what the real cost is after taking into consideration those items, then we're multiplying. At times, the weights, which are going to be there, are weighting between the debt and equity, to put it in perspective with regards to our capital structure. And then we're going to get the two point four for our weighted cost, then the common equity or retained earnings. We're going to say the cost after tax. There is no tax impact here. So after tax it would be the same amount because equity financing is 12 percent.

Not as straightforward to think about conceptually, because we're not paying in the form of interest when we issue equity. What we're getting instead is we're giving basically equity interest, interest in the equity in the earnings of the company and basically the retained earnings and the equity of the company and thinking about how that might grow in the future. So this becomes a little bit complex. This is an estimate for us to make. Once we get that number, then we can multiply that time to wait to put it into perspective, the weight between the equity, the debt and equity and our financing options. And that will give us then our seven point two percent.

If we add this up, the two point four and the seven point two is the nine point six. This would then be an attempt for us to get basically our required rate of return, our floor rate in order for us to be approving of a particular project. So if whether we be using the debt financing at the six percent or the common equity financing, the equity finance at the 12 percent, under this calculation, we want the floor to be our required rate of return to be the nine point six, and that allows us to basically look at different opportunities that we might have without without being distorted with regards to the weighting of what types of financing options should be there. And it gives us a quick look to be able to compare different types of things that we could be investing in.

So that's one kind of concept, one component that we can basically use for our investment decisions and cost of capital type of decisions. Now, also note that this formula up top doesn't include the preferred stock. So you could tack on preferred stock if the company has preferred stock, which would complicate things a little bit. I didn't adjust the formula. Well, just look at the table, what the table might look like. If you add the preferred stock, be something like this. You've got the debt at six percent. The weight is going to be 40 percent. Notice that these weights add up to one hundred percent because that's you know, these weights should add up to one hundred percent.

So the six percent tops, the 40 percent is the two point four percent preferred stock. Now, we're saying the cost after tax is 10 percent. The weight we're going to say is 10 percent. So 10 times 10, it's going to be the one percent. And then the common equity is going to be 12 percent times the weight of 50 percent or six percent adding those three up. That's going to give us nine point four. So we will go into the preferred stock as well and think about this calculation. So this is where our major focus will be going forward as we go forward and work through practice problems, calculating the debt and the cost of debt, the cost of equity, cost of preferred stock equity type of financing. You want to keep in mind how. You might want to measure that or think about that against other financing options and how you might put it into a whack type of calculation as well.

Cost of Debt

Now we're going to be focusing on components of that formula, drilling down into how we would get to particular components of this time, focusing on the cost of debt. So our cost of debt here, we're looking at basically the cost of debt here in the formula. As we do so, we want to keep in mind the basic idea of the formula, that being we're looking at financing options. There's two major categories for the financing option. We have debt financing.

We have equity financing. Once we think about the debt and equity financing, which are basically here and here in the formula, we got the debt and equity financing. We want to think about how we can compare those options, the debt and equity types of financing. You could think about how we can put them into the same type of format, comparing, as they say, apples to apples, same thing to same thing so that we could do that type of comparison. In order for that to happen, we need to realize on the debt financing side of things, we have the tax impact that will be taking place. So we'll talk a little bit more about that when we're figuring out this component of the formula.

Then once we have these numbers, we also want to take into consideration the current capital structure, which, as we saw in a prior chapter, is basically these weightings here. And that's going to be this part of the formula. So we want to keep that in mind as well. So basic idea. You want to keep in mind financing options to categories, debt, equity, financing type of options.

We want to be able to compare those two things and then we would like to put them into a formula to help us with our current capital structure as well. If you think about it with a table type of format, we have the cost after taxes, the cost of debt. This is what we're focusing on here. How do we get to that number now when we focus on it? In most of our practice problems, we will be taking into consideration the tax impact as we get to basically this number.

Meaning if I was trying to compare the cost of debt here to basically the cost of equity, then the cost of debt means that we're going to get money, we're going to get financing, we're going have to rent that money, in essence, meaning we're going to have to pay something on it, pay like the rent, which is called interest. So we're going have to pay interest on it. The interest that we pay is a deduction because it's a business type of expense and therefore we have kind of a benefit on the tax side of things. So what we would want to do is figure this as a percent after we get the benefit of the taxes that would be included. So it's not just going to be the interest rate, but we're going to get basically the after tax rate, which will be a benefit side of things.

So we want to get that percent so that we can then compare it to something like the cost of equity type of financing. Once we have those, once we have these numbers, then we can compare it to our current capital structure and are waiting here so that we can get a weighting effect as well and think about our financing options within that structure. So we're looking into the cost of debt then the interest rate for the company to raise capital through debt financing. So when you think about the cost of debt, you're basically thinking of the interest rate that's going to be applied. The problem here is the most complicated kind of problems with the cost of debt are usually related to the issuance of bonds. So the company issues bonds and they're going to then get money for the issuance of the bonds.

The question is, how much do those bonds cost the company? Well, they got you know, they got the money they're going to have to pay what? They're going to have to pay interest and then the interest is going to be deductible. So you have that component. So you would think it would be the interest rate. But then the bonds have this kind of funny thing where it's possible that we issued a bond for something other than the face amount of the bond, meaning issued at a premium or discount. And so that difference causes a problem as well, because now we have a market rate in essence, and we have the rate on the bond. Which rate do we use when we're thinking about the cost of the interest? And now we're generally going to use the market rate, the rate on the bond.

This will become more apparent as to why that would be the case when we actually do the calculations. But in essence, note what happens when the market rate is different from the rate on the bond, then we have to issue the bond at either a premium or a discount. And that difference that we're recording, the difference in the value that we're receiving compared to the face amount is basically interest. And therefore, even though we're paying out interest, that is going to be the amount based on the rate on the bond, our actual interest. If you take into consideration the fact that we sold it at a premium or discount, it will be reflected through that issuing at a premium or a discount. And there will be a tax impact over the life of.

The bond as we amortize that premium or discount, meaning we kind of expense it over time over the life of the bond, so we'll typically be using the market rate and and we might have to figure that out. So if you're looking at practice problems, they might give you the market rate, which could be called the yield to maturity, or they might give you the price. And we have to figure out the market rate. If that's the case, then these types of problems basically are going back to the prior chapter where we just looked at bonds basically and figuring out the price of the bond. Once you have that, then once you have basically the market rate, then you've got to take into consideration the tax impact.

So once we have the market rate, we've decided which rate we need to use. That then is not simply the cost of the debt when we want to compare to something else like equity, meaning if I was trying to compare, for example, to to type of debt items, then maybe it would be enough for me just to be using the market rate to look at the interest rate when I'm looking at two different items that have interest, both of those being tax deductible, because I'm comparing the same like to like same thing to the same thing. But if I'm trying to compare the financing options of something like debt financing, which has a tax impact to financing options which do not have a tax impact.

Now, I can't really compare those two unless I take into consideration the fact that one has a tax implication and the other does not. So that's what we basically have to do then the formula for that which you want to memorize and then you also want to kind of understand it intuitively, will look like this. Once we get the rate, we can then take a look at the tax implication as we do this in practice problems. I highly recommend going through practice problems, because when you simply learn this with a percent type of format, it can be a little abstract to learn that way. Oftentimes, if you were to work this out yourself, if you're trying to figure this out, you just figure this out. It's all intuitive.

You would probably set a debt amount like a thousand dollars and then figure out what the amount of the interest would be, what the tax rate would be, and then what the benefit would be from taxes. And then you can figure out the cost of debt after tax and a percentage basis. That's a longer method that is highly worth doing. It does give you more information. We will do that in the practice problems, but it's useful to jump right on a percentage basis and think about how we can get to the cost of debt after tax on a percentage basis. It will look something like this, the yield, which is basically the rate that you're paying and we're using if a bond, usually the market rate times one minus T, which is going to be the tax rate.

So it looks something like this. We've got the interest rate. If we imagine the interest rate, the rate that we're paying the market rate to be 10 percent, then we're going to take that 10 percent and multiply it times one or one hundred percent minus the tax rate, which we're assuming in this problem to be thirty five percent. So this would be one hundred percent or one. This would be zero point thirty five or thirty five percent. That means that we have sixty five percent left. Then we take the 10 percent times the sixty five percent we get the six point five. So what this means is that after taxes, the rate that this is costing us is really six point five, not 10 percent.

So the 10 percent is before taxes. After we take into account the tax benefit, we're at the six point five. Now, you can just memorize this. It's worth just memorizing, but you can also kind of mull it over so it makes sense to you here. Notice, if you're talking about looking at this one or one hundred percent, then that one hundred percent you can think about as the total difference in kind of a net income that would have the net tax impact, meaning the cost in this case of the interest. So this would be the effect on the net income, which would be the cost of the interest. And if I take that one hundred percent, minus the thirty five percent, which we imagine to be the tax rate and note, when you're thinking about the tax rate, you might be thinking, well, the tax rate is a progressive tax rate.

How did I get to thirty five percent when it's a progressive tax rate? Where do we get to this one number? Because it should be. Is it an average or is it the marginal tax rate usually will be using the marginal tax rate, even though there's a set a series of tax increases because like economists say, you know, we're making this decision on the margin. So we're imagining this decision at this point in time when we're already at the highest tax rate. So typically we can do kind of the easier thing here, take the highest tax rate instead of trying to do some kind of weighted average on the tax rate. Usually there could be some differences to that kind of concept.

But normally when you're making a next decision, the next decision from today, then you're looking at a decision that will have a tax impact at the highest rate, because that's where you currently are on the tax impact. So that means that basically of this difference that's going to happen, the one hundred percent of the change to net income resulting in the. We're basically going to get back thirty five percent in a tax benefit, right, we're going have to pay it in interest, but then we get paid back or we get to reduce our taxes by thirty five percent, given the fact that it's tax deductible. So that's why the one hundred percent minus the thirty five, that means the sixty five percent is really the items that of that tax benefit, the change to the net income, the interest that's going to have an impact. So now we're going to take that 65 percent times the 10 percent, which is the interest rate. And that's going to be our six point five.

Cost of Preferred Stock

You want to keep in mind the general idea of this concept, that being that we're looking at financing options, financing options that basically have two buckets within them, one being debt financing, one being, then the equity financing, then we can focus in on the specific components or the costs of debt financing and equity financing. We're now focusing on equity financing.

And when you think about equity financing, you're usually thinking about the common stock, the issuance of the common stock. When you issue the common stock, you're giving basically value in the company or ownership in the company claims to basically the retained earnings within the company. That could be a little bit more complex than, say, the preferred stock. So the preferred stock is a nice intro into basically the common stock. The preferred stock will differ from the debt financing because the debt financing, as we talked about in prior chapters, has a tax component to it. We pay the debt financing off with interest, typically the rent on the money, because that's an income statement amount. We're talking about an income tax.

There's a tax component. So this calculation here is going to be calculated after taxes so that we could compare it to something like equity financing. And then before we get into the equity financing of the common stock, which is a little bit more complex to estimate, it's useful to take the next step to go to a preferred stock. And maybe all companies may not have the preferred stock financing option. It might not be the first thing that comes to mind when you're thinking about equity financing. But if it's there, it's going to be a more simplified way of thinking due to the fact that the preferred stock doesn't have that same kind of voting rights and therefore the same kind of claim to the retained earnings. And what we could value with it will then be the dividends.

We can basically look at the dividends that will be paid in a similar fashion to the debt that would have interest paid to it and do a similar type of calculation. And it's even easier to some degree due to the fact that we don't have that tax impact with the equity financing because there's no impact on the income statement when we pay out the dividends on the preferred stock. Note that if you're looking at the preferred stock, we could add a component to the formula up here for the preferred stock and look at it on a formula basis. But I'm not going to do that here because basically I want to look at it as an intro into the common stock and think about the idea of having two major buckets when you're thinking about the financing, the debt financing and then the equity financing.

So the calculation for preferred stock will be similar to the debt financing here. But just note, there's another difference in it, and that is that the maturity date for the debt financing, even if you have long term bonds like 30 year bonds, is a maturity date. When you're talking about the preferred stock here on the equity financing, there's no real end date. You're paying dividends basically infinitely kind of into the future. So you have that difference that's going to be involved. So when we do these calculations to try to compare the same thing to the same thing, taking the after tax impact here, this kind of annual basis tax on average, you can think of the debt financing. And this is kind of the average annual for the preferred stock.

So you can kind of compare those out. But we're doing our best, the best we can to be able to compare them, noting that we still have to take some changes and differences into consideration. Once we have those, then we can apply the weights for our capital structure, as we saw in prior chapters, to get to the weighted average cost of capital. And that can help us with our financing, basically decisions here. So the cost of preferred stock, the preferred stock has a constant dividend payment with no end or maturity date. So, no, we're looking at dividends we have and we're thinking about valuing it. Then if we're thinking about the value of it or the cost, we think of our same concept of looking at those dividends out into basically infinity and then trying to present value what that would be.

So then we will divide dividend payments by net price, received priceless, any flotation costs, flotation costs of being the one time cost of the issuance. So we have this added kind of thing we want to take into consideration. It could be a little costly for the issuance of the stock. So we have to basically pay for the issuance of the stock, whatever kind of admin costs would be there. That cost is different from the dividend cost to us because it's a one time cost as opposed to the dividends, which are something we pay annually. We're going to assume it on an annual basis, basically, and forever in theory.

So this gives the rate of return to preferred stockholders and. Annual cost to the corporation because preferred stock is paid from equity, there is no tax impact or tax adjustment. And this is, Of course, one of the major differences with the debt financing, which is why we need to make that tax adjustment so we can compare this to the debt financing and try to look at similar types of things and then use that that information possibly in order to do the weighting so that we have the cost of preferred stock formula here. Cost of preferred stock will equal the annual dividends, the dividends that we're going to pay.

So we're imagining we issue the preferred stock in order to get financing, in order to get money. And then we're going to pay an annual dividend divided by the price of the preferred stock, minus the flotation, the price of the preferred stock. Obviously, what we got, that's what we got, minus the flotation cost. So it's going to be what it's going to cost us. The annual dividends per year, basically on an annual basis, minus the price of preferred stock. That's what we got, minus the flotation costs, because that's the one time cost that we had to give in order to issue the stock.

So it would look something like this. We have the annual dividend per share in a table type of format of eight. So we're assuming we pay eight dollars per share for the dividends then I would call it the net sales price down here. This is our net sales price, which is basically the sales price of the stock. We're assuming one 30. That's how much we sold it on the market for. We will sell these on the market. So, Of course, it will depend on what people are willing to pay for the preferred stock so that we set the price as high as we can in order to sell it on the market for that one thirty. And then we're estimating the flotation costs at two dollars. So it costs us two dollars to issue the stock. That two dollars is different from the dividend up top because the dividend is going to be an annual type of payment.

We're assuming it starts basically at the end of the year after the issuance, whereas the two dollars down down here is the one time payment. So if we were to sell it for one hundred and thirty, we got to pay the two dollars per share here upfront. So that means we're really only getting one twenty eight after the cost of the issuance. Then we can compare the eight dollars that we're going to pay on an annual basis to what we got, which isn't one thirty, even though we sold them for one thirty, but the one twenty eight after the one time issuance costs. And that'll give us the cost of preferred stock at the six point twenty five. So now that's six point twenty five.

We can compare to other types of financing options. Now if I want to compare it to debt financing options, then I have to make sure what I like on the debt side that I take into consideration the tax impact because there's a tax impact on the debt side. There's not a tax impact here because this is coming out of the dividends. That's still not perfect because we still kind of have this situation where, you know, you kind of have an equity type of type of interest versus the debt interest. You have a difference there. And we have a difference in basically our capital structure. So we might have put this into our weighted average cost of capital type of calculation.

And the dividends up top once again will in theory be paid forever. This is going to be paid forever versus the debt, which even if you're talking about long term debt of 30 years, then the dividends have some type of maturity date. So nothing's like a perfect comparison. There are different things, but we want to make them as much as possible to be on a comparable basis so that we can make the best decision we can based on the best information we could put together.

Cost of Common Equity

Conceptually, we're focusing in on a particular component, this time being the cost of equity which would be here and the cost of equity down below as well as we think of these practice problems, we always want to have in the back of our mind the financing options, financing, taking basically two primary categories, two primary buckets, that being debt financing and equity financing. We're focusing now on the equity financing, the equity financing, not having the same kind of tax impact as debt financing.

That's one of the differences between debt and equity financing. So we first want to get our financing options into a way that we can compare them as best we can, put them in a comparable type of format and then take into consideration our weights. And so what we'll be focusing on now is this particular component. How do we get to that number so that we can then use it basically in our weights and or compare it to other financing options with maybe the debt financing options as well. So we started off thinking about the debt financing options. The cost of debt is fairly straightforward because it's typically interest.

So we pay interest or rent on what we borrow, but there's a tax impact that we have to take into consideration. And we particularly need to take that into consideration with debt financing if we want to compare that then to equity financing. Because one of the more simplified things about equity financing is that we don't have that kind of situation with the tax impact on it. So if I'm trying to compare these two situations, the two financing options and trying to make them as likely as possible to make a good comparison, I need to take into consideration the tax implication on the debt side, which is not on the equity side. When thinking about the equity side, we talked last time about preferred stock, which is probably the less common component, and it's not included really in our formula up top.

But it's a good intro into the equity financing because it takes, you know, the difference between the debt without the tax impact, without being as complicated to try to predict what the common stock kind of issuance would be in that the preferred stock is going to be more simplified. We don't have the same kind of concept of ownership and therefore the like retained earnings allocation to the preferred stock. And we can therefore value our dividend payments in a similar way we do with the debt financing. We saw, however, that there is a difference in that the dividend payments for preferred stock could be imagined to basically go on forever, whereas the amount of interest for debt would stop at some point in time, even if it's a long bond, like a 30 year type of bond.

So we can take those same concepts with the preferred stock and then go to the common stock. But then we have the added complication that we have to put in place. How do we value how we get to our cost of the common stock? So when we issue the common stock we're thinking about, we're issuing basically claims to the retained earnings, the net value ownership, interest, voting rights to the common stockholders. So basically we have to take into consideration the dividends that we're going to pay. We can think about it that way conceptually. We can think about it as basically the dividends out into infinity kind of in the future, trying to basically present value what that would be.

And that's one way we can basically visualize how we get to the common equity. But you can see that given the fact that we're basically given ownership interest into the organization, it's a bit more complex of a valuation than the preferred stock. Once we have that valuation, then we can do our comparison to the debt here and then we can multiply it. Times are ways to get our weighted average cost of capital and so on. But again, there's going to be more estimates, most likely with the common equity than the other kind of components to get to this basic number. So the cost of the common equity valuation approach. So this is going to be the valuation approach can be more complex as we consider pricing and performance demands of current and future stockholders.

So we're going to look at the pricing and performance considerations into the future. Quite difficult when you're thinking about someone who has an equity interest because that's a piece or a valuation of the entire company basically as a whole, because it's kind of like an ownership interest. So it's a larger thing that you're trying to estimate. So we could take the dividend valuation model. Look, we have the price of the stock today. This is on a percentage basis equal to the dividends at the end of the year. This would be similar to comparing it to debt when we're talking about interest basically on an annual basis on the preferred stock, which has the dividends as well, divided by the required rate of return, which is kind of like the discount rate.

Minus the constant growth rate in dividends, these bottom two numbers, Of course, are something that we're projecting out into the future and therefore those are going to be estimates, projections in order to get to our calculation. Another method we could use for the cost of common equity capital asset pricing model, otherwise known as APM. We're not going to go into a lot of practice problems on the calculation here. But just keep in mind this model as well. We might talk about it in future chapters. It's going to be reliant on more kinds of market based information. So that required a return on common stock equal to R.F. plus B times K.M.

minus R.F. where RF is equal to the risk free rate of return. That's kind of like our baseline there, which is often the rate on the Treasury Bill securities, which is where you could find that rate b Bayti coefficient measures the historical volatility of an individual stock return related to an index. So again, we're showing the relationship to an index, which again is kind of like a market based item, an average kind of system. And then K.M. being equal to the return of the market, measured by an approach, an approximate index, once again being relied on an approximate index for our calculation here, cost of retained earnings, capital sources from common stock equity. We have the external source and internal sources, external sources, the purchase of new shares.

So when we issue the shares, that's going to be one of the sources for the cost of the retained earnings. The internal source would be, Of course, the earnings less distributions. So remember, when we're thinking about the issuance of the common stock, you're basically thinking from an accounting standpoint or valuation standpoint, reevaluating our accounting equation assets minus liabilities is equity issuance of the shares is then providing an ownership interest, an internship, ownership of the equity net value of the corporation. So the external source would then be us issuing the shares, receiving funds for that on the internal side of things. We then have the earnings whenever we make earnings on the income statement, those earnings are then increasing.

The the retained earnings, the retained earnings on the balance sheet is what's showing us at a particular point in time the accumulation of earnings which are shown on the income statement, the income statement showing the performance to get to the end point, which is the balance sheet, the retained earnings representing those earnings over time that have been accumulated, which are part of the value of the company. And then we could distribute some of that in the form of dividends. So the dividends represent us reducing the retained earnings. What has grown over the company over time through business generation of revenue.

And we're taking that value and giving it to the owners in the form of dividends, those being similar to distributions. So when you're thinking about the breakout of an equity kind of chapter on the balance sheet, the whole equity chapter as a whole, you're thinking that that's kind of like the value of the company assets, minus liabilities, basically being the value equity chapter and then the equity chapter. We can then say, well, if there's a purchase, if we sell the stocks, that's going to be us. That represents the common stock, represents us selling ownership, interest in basically the company claim to the retained earnings and receiving then the funds related to that from the external source.

And then the retained earnings portion represents the portion of the income that has been accumulated into the company that has not yet been distributed out in the form of dividends. So retained earnings belong to stockholders and are either paid as dividends or reinvested. So the retained earnings is part of the value of the organization. Stockholders are owners of the organization. At some point in time, the owners of the organization should be getting value they own that retained earnings, their portion related to their shares of the stock. And at some point in time, we can imagine that value to be distributed to the owners in some way, shape or form over the lifetime of the company in the form of dividends.

Or we can imagine basically, Of course, the value of the company going up as the dividends are not paid out and being reinvested, hopefully in order to generate a higher return, increasing the value of the company. So that's going to be the general overall cost of retained earnings. So if we want to calculate the cost of the retained earnings, we're going to be looking at this on a percentage type of basis. Cost of retained earnings is equal to the rate of return on the company's common common cost. The formula below represents the required rate of return on common stock and the cost of equity in the form of retained earnings.

So the cost of common equity in the form of retained earnings. We're going to calculate this and call this. The cost of retained earnings will change it slightly in the future. Chapter to take into consideration the flook. Haitian costs to distribute the stock out. This is going to be the dividend at the end of the first year, so now we're just looking at the dividend. At the end of the first year, we're going to divide that by the price of the stock. The price of the stock is, Of course, what we sell the stock for. We would be issuing the stock onto the stock market. Remember, when you think about purchasing and selling on the stock market, most purchases and sales aren't coming from the company. They're being sold between each other on a publicly traded exchange.

And in this case we're talking about the company itself issuing the stock. Therefore, the stock price is what the company will receive. They will still issue it at the market price. They're going to sell it for as much as they can, but then that money is going to be going to the company. So we're taking a look at the dividend at the end of the year. That's what we're going to have to pay out. That's a similar type of calculation we saw with the debt financing when we're looking at interest on a yearly basis or with the preferred stock divided by the price. But then we need to add to that the constant growth rate of the dividends, and that's going to take into consideration kind of the increase in the valuation of the company as well.

So if we look at the calculation down below, it might help us to make sense of this. We have the dividends per share, we're going to say four dollars. That's what we're going to be paying out. We're going to stay here annually. And then we divide that by the common stock price, which is going to be the 90 dollars that's going to give us our four point four four. This is a similar calculation as with the preferred stock, also similar to the debt. When we're trying to come up with this percent with the debt, we would then have to take into consideration tax impact. There's no tax impact here. We don't have to worry about that. But we also have the growth kind of component that we need to take into consideration.

And this is where the big estimate would be, you know, in this kind of calculation, that would be the constant growth rate of the dividends that we would have to estimate what the constant growth rate of the dividends would be, and then add that to our four point four four to come up with our cost of the retained earnings, something that we can then see on a percentage basis and possibly use it to compare then to other types of financing methods, possibly something like debt financing. So we could also have the cost of common stock. This is going to be a similar calculation here, but now we're going to take into consideration the flotation costs, the cost of us issuing the stock so we have the greater than the cost of retained earnings due to flotation costs. These are the distribution costs that we're going to add into.

The calculation is the required rate of return for the current shareholders. So when we're thinking about our rate of return for the current shareholders, we want to take into consideration then the flotation cost, the cost of common equity in the form of retained earnings, you'll recall, is what we just looked at, dividends at the end of the year, dividends at the end of the first year, divided by the price, plus the constant growth rate of dividends. One change now here. That's going to be the flotation costs in our formula for the cost of common stock, which is going to be the dividends at the end of the first year. Same thing. But instead of dividing by the price of the stock only, we're going to take the price of the stock minus the flotation costs, the flotation costs being that one time thing, because this is not something that we're going to pay annually. Right.

It's just the cost of us issuing the stocks as we first issued them. So it's a one time cost. So instead of getting the price into the company, we're really getting the price minus that one time costs. And then we will do the same thing and add them to the constant growth rate of dividends. So it looks something like this and a table type of format. It's going to be the dividends per share. We're going to say it's four dollars the net price. Now, I'm going to calculate this bottom calculation. Common stock price was ninety dollars minus the flotation cost. Here the flotation costs are different from the dividends that we're going to have to pay. Dividends paid annually, flotation costs paid one time.

Therefore, if we issue the stock for ninety dollars on the market, someone paid ninety dollars. But we had to pay someone to get those stocks out of the three dollars, meaning we're really getting eighty seven dollars on what I would call like a net price. So if we now take the four dollars divided by the eighty seven we get the four point six, then we're in the same situation we were at before where we'd need to then calculate and add the constant growth rate of dividends, that being the six percent to get to the ten point six. Now, if you kind of move us over, obviously once again, the six percent is going to be some type of estimate here. You can kind of try to think about why this makes sense in your mind.

You could basically think that this four point six is the similar calculation of what we're paying annually as compared to what we're going to be receiving. And then this six percent, we're trying to basically you can think about it as a present value in the future cash flows that we basically thought about before, meaning you can conceptually think about the ownership of the company being the equity. The equity is going to be distributed over the lifetime in some way in the form of dividends and try to basically present value this. Right. So this is you can think about this as a.

To think about the return that would be what we have to give back in terms of the dividends and this is an attempt to basically then value the growth on the equity, on the the valuation side of things, but use it as a cash flow method to do so. But in any case, then we get to the ten point six to ten point six billion, something that we have a percent now that we can then compare it to other financing options, such as the debt financing. Once again, it's not perfect because when we think about the debt financing, we do have certain differences, meaning, for example, the debt financing.

We're comparing interest up top. And the interest is something paid annually. But even though we can kind of take into consideration the tax impact of it, even after that, we have a maturity date for the debt financing for bonds, even if it's a long maturity date out into the future. This for dollars of dividends, in theory, can go on basically forever. And then, Of course, we have the added complication down here of the expected growth calculation to know exactly what that is. That's a more complex type of calculation than a dividend where you basically have a fixed set of terms. It can be a little complicated to figure out the tax, the after tax impact, but there's less unknowns there than, you know, trying to value the company and get that expected growth rate.

The Optimal Capital Structure

Now we're going to go into a little bit more detail about the wacky formula in concept and why this weighted average component is going to be important. In other words, we started off in general thinking about the components of this formula, breaking them out, the financing of the organization into two main categories, that being debt financing and equity financing, thinking about the concept of the weighting, which includes this part of the calculation, the concept of the weighted here.

And then we consider them in a table format, considering the current weighting as well. Then we went into more detail to think about the calculation for the cost of debt and equity, which is going to be this component of the equation and this component of the equation. And in the table we calculate these then down below as well. And then we think about our once we plug that into the formula, we're taking into consideration the cost of debt and the cost of equity in terms that are somewhat comparable. And we're basically weighting them, taking into consideration our current capital structure to give us our whack our weighted average cost of capital, which is the minimum rate that would be kind of like our discount rate or our expected rate of return for particular projects.

So that's going to be the calculations of it. Let's think about why that works a little bit more in depth. We thought about how to get to these particular components. Now we're kind of thinking about why or what is the optimal weights between basically the debt and equity financing a little bit in more depth as to why the wack formula would be put together the way it be put together. So remember, the concept here is we have the assets. This is basically our balance sheet that we have. How do we finance those assets? We have debt or equity type of financing. Typically, if we had no debt, we would finance it through equity, through the operations of the organization and through the selling of stocks and so on.

And then we have the debt up here that we could also finance by taking out loans and bonds. But the debt and the debt is usually considered to be cheaper or could be cheap financing options for the debt, and therefore there could be an optimal structure between the debt and equity. So in other words, as debt goes up, we have certain risks that are going to be increasing with the debt and we could then have a risk of bankruptcy and also the return that the shareholders are going to want when they have more risk due to the fact of debt increasing could impact the required rate of return on the equity side of things. So, Of course, the question then is how much debt to be taken on equity is usually going to be more expensive versus the debt, but then as the debt increases, the risk is going to increase. What's going to basically be the optimal level? That's when we get into our weighted average cost of capital, the whack type of calculation as a way to get to that nice spot for the maximum types of returns.

Our goal then is to maintain a minimum cost of capital by financing between the options of debt, preferred stock and common stock. Now we're going to be focusing mainly here on debt and the common stock, the preferred stock being another kind of equity financing. But we want to basically think of that as a kind of leading into a simplified way to get into the common stock. But conceptually, let's think of our two categories, that being debt financing and then equity financing. So the factor for the capital mix decision is assessing the current capital structure. So we want to think about what the current capital structure is and then what's taking that into consideration, deciding if the current structure is optimal as we make decisions going forward in the future for financing options between the debt and equity. Here we are in our graph.

We have the cost of capital percent on the vertical axis. We have the debt asset ratio on the horizontal lines including the cost of equity, weighted average cost of capital and the cost of debt. We're focusing on the weighted average cost of capital. We could see that this is a U. Shaped line, and where we would like to be is at the bottom point of this line that then minimizes the cost of capital per cent. So when you think about this, just in terms of a question, if there's a test question on it or you're thinking about this just in terms of a graph, theoretically, then Of course we're going to say, well, I want to minimize the cost of capital percent. I want to be at this minimum point, which is basically the idea of our weighted average cost of capital type of calculation. And then you get into more depth in terms of like, well, why would that be the case? And it can get quite complex.

And when. Think about, you know, why would that be the case, but a short answer, some would say, would be that it's going to be a tax impact would be the result of this, because when you pull in the debt, then you have that tax implication with regards to the debt making the debt cheaper. So, for example, there is an argument that would say something like this. If you had a world with basically no taxes and you're looking at the cost of equity as you raise debt, as you raise the debt, it might look something like this. So the cost of equity then increasing as the debt, then going up, cost of equity, then increasing due to the fact that as debt goes up, the people that are the shareholders are going to to want to have a higher return based on a higher required return, based on the more risk that is going up as the debt goes up.

The argument then being that the weighted average cost of capital in that situation would be basically a straight line in that situation, because as the debt goes up, it's going to be counterbalanced off by the increase in the required rate of return in a world with no taxes. But if you're talking about a world with taxes, then we actually have a decrease. You're going to end up in the result with as you take on the debt, you then have the weighted average cost of capital decreasing. That would be beneficial then resulting in returns being greater for the shareholders as you take on debt to some point in time. And then it's going to go back up again.

Now, that counterbalancing, why would that happen? What does that counterbalancing take place where you got the tax impact? Because obviously, again, the interest is going to be deductible for the taxes. But then at some point in time, then as you take on more debt people, the shareholders are going to want that higher return. And at some point in time, also you could get to where the cost of debt increases because the risk goes up and you could call that like the risk of bankruptcy. If people have less faith that the debt will be able to be repaid, then the required rate of return will go up. And at some point in time, the agencies that are rating you could go down from like a triple-A rating to a AAA rating or something like that, which would result in more risk. The more risk would actually increase the interest rates.

So now you have a situation where the interest rates on the debt could then go up. So at this point in time, when you get over to this side, increasing the debt past a certain point, you have a greater risk, let's say a bankruptcy that could happen. And once the wheels start turning on the bankruptcy side of things, it can get out of control fairly quickly because, again, if your rating agency goes down or something like that and then your cost of debt then increases, that could be a problem. So what you want to do to maximize that goal then would be to be somewhere down here to take on the debt to maximize. But, B, possibly this is a fairly flat point of the curve somewhere on this side, maybe of the flat point of the curve to be more safe, but still take on the debt in order to maximize the return.

So that's kind of conceptually what's happening with the idea of the weighted average of the weight between the debt and the equity? The debt is often something that could be cheaper. But you want to get that basically ideal weighting between the two, that nice balance between the two to maximize. So again, what you want to basically know is like a test question or something like that, you want to know where this point is going to be. If you want to, you know, break this down theory wise, like look at models. There's a lot of information in terms of exactly why this would be the case and calculations for it can get somewhat complex.

So it's interesting to see that. But the basic idea we got, the two the two components that we can use for the financing of the organization, debt equity, there's some kind of ideal component for some reasons. And some of those reasons may be the tax impact, although it can get quite complex once you start digging into it. And your ideal point would be, although not always the easiest thing to calculate, but theoretically makes sense to the ideal point would be some ideal mix between the two and the weighted average cost of capital is an attempt to find that point, that range. So companies may sell common stock when prices are high to minimize the cost of equity. A balance between equity and debt is needed to get the minimum cost of capital.

That's going to be the objective capital budgeting decisions. The cost of capital for each source of funds is necessary for a good budgeting decision. So we've got to figure out what the cost of the capital is for the different sources. The required rate of return equals the weighted average cost of capital, otherwise known as the whack that's going to be. Are required rates of return and then the stock price for the company should increase or at least stay the same as long as the company earns the cost of capital. So as long as the company is making good decisions and earning then their cost of capital, you would think that would be representative of people saying that the company is doing a good job and earning what they should and taking on the financing that is appropriate and therefore the stock either stays the same or hopefully increases due to that. The market then reflects in the decision making process of the organization.

Cost of Debt After Tax Prob 1

We have our information up top. We'll go through the calculations then down below for them. Keeping in mind when we're thinking about this topic here, we're thinking about financing options for an organization. You can categorize financing options, how they're going to basically finance their operations, and get money into different categories. One debt and two equity. We're going to be focusing on debt here. When we think about debt, then the typical thing that we have to pay with regards to debt, the cost of the debt is the rent on the purchasing power of the money that we have to pay to whoever we basically got the money from. And that is going to be called interest.

So we have interest, typically straightforward to calculate, although there could be different formats of how the interest will be paid, the further complication here will be taxes. Taxes are always complicating the situation. We're dealing with something that will be on the income statement. It's an income tax that we're talking about. Therefore it will have a tax impact. Taxes are always backwards with regards to what we would normally be thinking in general, meaning normally we don't like interest because that's like paying rent on the purchasing power of money. Not good, but for taxes, it's a good deduction.

Therefore, we have this kind of counterbalancing impact in terms of the impact in total when we take into consideration taxes with regards to debt financing, with equity financing, we don't have that same kind of situation because we have a difference. It's not something that's going to have a tax impact. It's not an income statement type of transaction. So keep that in mind. We'll get into that more later. So we're going to say the interest rate, let's say, is five percent and the tax rate is thirty percent. Let's not even think about the debt first. Let's just think about the rates. And then you could basically think about and figure what the cost of debt after tax on a percentage basis would be, just simply with the rates now then we'll add the one hundred thousand and just add the debt, because I think intuitively many people would understand this better by basically having the debt and then calculating it in that format.

But let's first do this interest calculation. This is very important to have. Like just in your mind, you kind of just want to memorize the formula, but you also just want to intuitively understand what's going on as well. So that'll help you to memorize it. So we're going to say the cost of debt after taxes calculation, we're going to say the interest rate is going to be the five percent and then we're going to take one minus the tax rate. So the tax rate is thirty percent. Remember that when we talk about the tax rate, we have a progressive tax system, meaning as your income goes up, the tax rate could go up. So it could be more or less progressive in terms of the system. But also note, when you're making decisions, you're often making them on, as economists call the margin, meaning the last decision that you're basically making.

Therefore, you might be making the decision and just considering your highest tax rate, because that's going to be the one that has the most impact on your last decision. However, it could be more complex than that in some situations if it could have an impact on multiple different tax rates. But that's one reason why we could basically use one tax rate here that we're going to say we're probably using the high tax rate, not the average tax rate, most likely because we're making our decision at the margin. That's where our tax is at that point. So then we're going to have the one and then the tax rates. So we're taking one minus the tax rate.

You could think of the one, Of course, one hundred percent or one minus the tax rate, which you could think of as point three or thirty percent, that would then give us the 70 percent. So then we take the 70 percent times the interest rate of five percent, and that's going to give us our three point five. So the basic formula you have is the five percent interest rate times one minus the tax rate. So you kind of just want to memorize that. But if you understand it intuitively, you don't really even need to memorize it. You're basically kind of seeing what's happening intuitively. So it could be a little bit confusing when you think about this with no actual debt. No. That you're basically calculating. But here, Of course, we have the interest rate, which would be the interest rate times the debt.

That would be normal. Debt that we would calculate, but then we got to take into consideration we have a tax impact for the deductible portion, what's the relation of the tax impact? Well, if we had one hundred percent of the tax impact, which basically we can think about as the deduction that you would get for the interest rate, that would be the impact on the income statement, basically on net income. And then we subtract out the tax rate, the 30 percent that tax rate, the 30 percent of it is the amount that we can kind of think that we're going to reverse due to the tax impact. In other words, we're going to have to pay the interest of that amount, which is not good, because we have to pay it, but we're going to get a tax benefit. In other words, we kind of get it back in some ways.

So that leaves us with 70 percent. That's not going to be basically impacted or reversed out with taxes. So now we've got a 70 percent interest rate of five percent. That means that we have the cost of debt after taxes percent at the three point five percent. So when we think of the cost of the debt, then normally we think, well, the cost of the debt is the five percent interest we have to pay, just like we would think the cost of the rent that we pay on a building is the annual rent that we pay or something like that. The cost of the debt would be five percent. But if you kind of compare that to other options for financing, I need something more specific. I'd like to take into consideration the tax impact because I get to deduct the taxes.

And if I think about other options of financing, such as equity financing, I don't have to think about the taxes. Therefore, that's going to be a relevant issue with my decision making process between the financing decisions. So I need to get my tax after tax rate, which would be the three point five. So that's going to be the three point five after tax. So we can compare that to other options of financing without even figuring out the amount of financing we need. The amount in this case is like a loan or something like that, or the debt that we would then be issuing. But it's useful to then calculate what we would issue. Most people, I would think, would benefit by actually plugging in one hundred thousand or some kind of amount that you figure that you're going to be borrowing or issuing debt in some type of way.

And then think about this intuitively in terms of what is going to be the amount you're going to be paying in interest, what's going to be the benefit on the taxes. So let's do that. Now, that would be something like this. I think this is useful to do. We do this in Excel, too. So you could take a look at that. If I was seeing this problem up top and I'm not fully understanding it in my mind or I want to prove it to myself, I might go through a calculation like this. I'd say, well, alright then. The interest calculation is five percent. We're assuming that's an annual rate here. So if I take the debt of one hundred thousand, which we could just make up, put in some debt, no, we're assuming one hundred thousand times the five percent. If that was the case, then we would be paying interest of five thousand dollars. That would be the normal cost that we would have for five thousand.

But then there's a tax impact that five thousand is going to be deductible and therefore we're going to get a tax benefit of deducting the interest. Remember, taxes are completely backwards. And so we got to say, all right, well, now there's a tax benefit. If we had the tax benefit, we can take that deductible interest, which is now an expense to us. Which or a deduction. An expense which would be kind of like a business deduction times the tax rate, which we're saying is 30 percent. It's going to have an impact of 30 percent. Therefore, we have a tax benefit of five thousand times 30 percent or one thousand five hundred.

So if we were borrowing one hundred thousand and five percent, we would be paying five thousand but thirty percent of that five thousand. We kind of get back in a way with the taxes because we get to deduct it and get a tax benefit. So the five thousand minus the one thousand five hundred leaves us with the cost of debt after taxes on a dollar basis of the three thousand five hundred. So then I got to thinking, well, I would like to see it on a percentage basis so we can say, all right, well then let's just take the cost of debt after tax on a percent base. Let's take that cost of debt after taxes to three thousand five hundred. Compare it to the debt itself. The one hundred thousand three thousand five hundred divided by one hundred thousand would then give us the three point five percent.

So that's the cost of debt after tax on a percentage basis. So you can get to it nice and quickly. Up top with this formula here, interest times one minus the rate and then intuitively you can kind of prove it to yourself by doing the normal type of calculation. You can imagine this being like on a tax return here, you know, that you would be basically doing in figuring that say, OK, yeah, that kind of rings true to me. Now, when you're doing an actual calculation, you might shorten this out. And if you are thinking about a situation where you have a one hundred thousand dollar debt, that or issuance or debt that you're going to take on in some way.

To finance the company, you might do the calculation, something like this one hundred thousand, and then figure out the cost of debt after tax percent, which is going to be just like the first calculation we had, which is the five percent, and then take into consideration the tax effect, one minus the tax rate. This is the first calculation we did, right, five percent. The rate times one minus the tax rate, that would be one hundred percent minus 30 percent or one minus point three, giving us point seven or 70 percent. And then if we multiply that out the five percent times to 70 percent we get the three point five. Remember to be careful about decimals and whatnot, point five times the point. Seven what gives us the point.

Oh, three, five. Or if we make it a percent, three point five percent, then if we take that three point five percent, we can then multiply it times the one hundred thousand times and we get the three thousand five hundred, the three thousand five hundred. And you note this is a much quicker calculation that I can deal with an actual number. So up top we did the calculation. Just thinking about the percent. You want to basically memorize this formula. Understand it intuitively. That's going to be the rate times one minus the tax rate. And then you can apply that out to actual numbers, the financing being the one hundred thousand in this case, instead of doing this longer calculation up top, which I think is useful to do and gives you more information.

But if you're trying to do a quick calculation and present it to somebody, then you can also do a nice quick calculation here by taking the rate times one minus the tax rate. And obviously, if you're presenting to somebody here, what I would do normally is basically calculate this out. If someone doesn't really understand this thing that we're talking about here, it can be a little difficult to explain basically on a percent basis. Then I would be ready for that and say, OK, let's break it out this way. And I think this just intuitively will make more sense to people when they have the attention span to go through, the longer the longer calculation for it. So I highly recommend doing this kind of practice problems in Excel. We have multiple problems in Excel, rework them multiple times and just get a good feel for them.

Cost of Debt After Tax Prob. 2

We have our information up top. We're going to go through those calculations down below. We're talking about the financing options for an organization, for a company, for example. Those financing options typically being in two main categories: debt financing, equity financing, focusing here on the debt financing. Remembering that when thinking about the debt financing, we also have to be considering the tax impact because the major cost of the debt financing is something that impacts the income statement and therefore has a tax effect. That being interest, the cost, the interest, that being an expense and expense is bad normally, but for taxes, good taxes, backwards taxes .

Therefore, we have to consider the tax impact so that we can compare financing options from something like debt financing to equity financing, which doesn't have that kind of tax impact, but has different kinds of costs and benefits that we need to consider. All right. So we have our information. Up top companies can issue the debt. The interest rate will consider an annual rate here, 12 percent. The tax rate. Twenty six percent. Remember, when we're thinking about the tax rate, we have a progressive tax system. So you might say, hey, how do you get one rate? Where do we take the average rate or something like that? Note that oftentimes we're making a decision on the margin. As economists say, that means it's the last rate that we're looking at because that's where we are at this point in time.

We're paying the last dollar, the highest tax rate on it. Making a decision at this time at the margin means we're typically making a decision that will impact the highest tax rate. So we may then use that one, although it can't get more complex and nuanced depending on the size and circumstance. Then we have the debt down below one hundred thousand. We're going to do our calculation first, not considering the debt at all. And we're going to try to think about this, basically saying I would like to just look at the percentage cost and see if we can then compare that to different options up top and then consider the debt. It's often useful to add the debt in the calculation to better understand what the actual calculation is doing. So first of all, calculate it without the debt at all.

We're looking for the cost of debt after tax. You basically want to memorize this formula, but you also want to know it intuitively. So we have the tax rate, we're going to say to 12 percent annually. Then you're going to take that time one minus the I'm sorry, not the tax rate. We have an interest rate of 12 percent. Then we're going to take that time one minus the tax rate. There's one minus the tax rate, which is going to be twenty six percent. You could think of it as one hundred percent, minus twenty six percent or one minus point to six. That's going to give us our point seventy four or seventy four percent. We're going to take that and multiply it times the twelve, the interest rate to get the eight point eight eight percent, thereby saying that after taxes, the percentage basically the cost of debt after taxes on a percentage basis is not 12 percent the interest rate, but the eight point eighty eight percent.

And then we can compare that to other options, possibly helping us to compare it to two options that don't have a tax impact, such as the equity options. If we consider this, then normally you want to kind of understand this, just memorize the formula, but also it'll be easier to memorize if understood. We're taking the interest rate. Normally, the interest rate times the amount of the debt, if we're talking annual rate, would give us the amount that we're going to pay. But then we have that. That's the cost of the debt. But then we have that tax impact. What's the tax impact on basically a percentage basis? Well, if we think about the change in the income statement, because we're talking about an income statement tax, we're talking about the change in the income statement, which is basically the cost of the expense.

If we think about one hundred percent of that, minus the twenty six percent, the twenty six percent being the tax rate that we are then applying, that means that we're basically going to get like twenty six back in some way, meaning we're going to pay it in interest. But twenty six percent of it, we're kind of getting back due to the fact that it's going to wash out in our taxes. We can think about it as the IRS kind of paying it back or lowering our tax bill by that amount. Therefore the seventy four percent is the amount that's actually going to be. It Affected me, and we're going have to pay for it and we're not going to get it back basically in taxes, you can think about it that way. So if we take the 74 percent times to 12 percent, we're talking about an after tax impact of the eight point eighty eight.

So when we're comparing something that doesn't have a tax impact, such as financing through equity, it's useful for us to be comparing the same thing to the same thing, using possibly the rate of this eight point eighty eight. So then it's useful then to think about this in terms of the one hundred thousand, let's plug the debt in. Oftentimes this calculation, people just memorize it, but they don't really understand it. If you then wanted to break it out in your mind, if you were actually to do this intuitively, you'd probably do something like this, which is worthwhile doing. You'd say, hey, let's just add a debt amount here, say one hundred thousand and calculate what the cost would be after tax on an actual dollar amount basis and then see what the percent basis would be.

So we could say, all right, well, if I just assume debt that we're going to have is one hundred thousand debt, one hundred thousand times the cost of debt, the 12 percent, that's how much we're actually going to have to pay if it's an annual rate, meaning we're going to pay the twelve. That's not good. Money's going out the door of the 12000. That's the cost. That's the rent on us getting the purchasing power of one hundred thousand by taking it from someone else who's willing to give it to us because we're going to pay the rent on it, which is 12 percent of the dollar amount, twelve thousand. Then we have the tax benefit, which is going to be the fact that we get to deduct this twelve thousand most likely.

And that means that we get the twelve thousand times the twenty six percent, which is going to be the tax rate that we're using at the margin, possibly then being the highest tax rate, the twelve thousand times to twenty six percent, giving us the three thousand one hundred and twenty. So we're paying twelve thousand to the, to the debtor who we borrowed from in some way, shape or form. And then we're getting back however or lowering our tax bill by the three thousand one twenty four paying it. So the twelve thousand minus to three thousand one twenty gives us the eight thousand eighty, which is the actual basically after tax caused the debt, not taking on a not on a percentage basis. Right. That's the after tax on a dollar basis. So then what's, what is it on a percentage basis?

Well now we can say alright well then we'll just going to take that eight eight eight. Oh that's the actual dollar value cost divided by the original debt. One hundred thousand. That then gets us back to the eight eighty eight. There's the eight eighty eight. This exercise is useful to do. To better understand this. I recommend doing it in Excel multiple times. However, in practice, in book problems and whatnot, you'd rather not have to go through this whole process of making up a number or this or that and just memorize the formula. However, it's easier to memorize the formula if you understand the formula.

Now, once you have this in practice, you might then ask the question as what if we had this one hundred thousand dollar debt? You know, what would the cost after tax cost be? And I can get there more quickly. I'm looking to get to this eight thousand eight eighty. Instead of doing this double kind of calculation, we can get there a little bit more quickly, which could be easier for us to do. If we understand it intuitively. It could be easier for us to present. But if you do this, it also can be a little less intuitive. So if I was to present something, you might do it this way. We'd say, here's the debt, the one hundred thousand, and then we're taking the cost of debt after taxes. We're multiplying at times. That formula, which would be the interest rate times one minus the tax rate or one hundred percent. Twenty six percent or seventy four percent.

So interest rate times one minus the tax rate gives us then the eight point eighty eight. If we have then the eight point eighty eight. That's the after tax cost of the debt times the one hundred thousand that then gets us the eight thousand eighty. So the same thing we did up top here but a little bit, a little bit quicker because we did our quick little calculation that you kind of want to memorize here for it. Now, if you were to present this, I would present this. And if someone asks you, like, what does this mean in the middle? I don't understand this kind of calculation. It's a little difficult to calculate or interpret it, you know, just with %s. If you then break out this calculation, then I think this is a little bit more intuitive just for anybody to basically see what is actually going on. So I would keep that in the back of my chapters or something like that.

Have that ready if someone has questions about it, if it was something like that. So then if we do this again, let's do it again. Let's say, well, let's say the interest rate is 10 percent, the tax rate is thirty two percent. The debt is one hundred thousand. First, we're going to calculate it just with the rates. This is the formula that you want to memorize. It's going to be then the interest rate, ten percent times one minus the tax rate, one minus the tax rate or one hundred percent minus whatever the percent of the taxes. So you could say one minus point to three or one hundred percent, minus the thirty two percent is going to give us the sixty eight percent and then we simply take the rate times that.

Sixty eight percent would mean that. Of the debt costing us the 10 percent, which is actually the interest we will pay after taxes due to the tax benefit, we will then actually have an after tax rate of six point eight percent, which we can then possibly compare to other options, possibly equity options, which don't have that same kind of tax impact. Comparing them, as they say, apples to apples or the same thing to the same thing, because comparing different things is not very helpful. Useful usually, although it could be fun, I guess. But in the case now, let's do the same thing with the one hundred thousand here. One hundred thousand, we're going to say here's the interest we got the debt times, the times, the rate. That means that we would have then the debt of the 10000.

This is how most people would probably work this out in their mind if they were just doing it themselves. And they're just saying, let me see if I can make sense of this. We're going to take the one hundred thousand times that 10 percent is ten thousand. That's how much interest we're going to pay. And then there's a tax benefit because I get to deduct that ten thousand. So then I get a tax benefit expense or a deduction times the highest tax rate, because we're going to say this is happening on the margin at this point in time. Decisions happening now at the end, when we're already at the tax rate of thirty two percent, we're considering possibly our highest tax rate. Ten thousand times at thirty two percent means we're going to get a lower bill of our taxes due to us taking on the debt of three thousand two hundred. So ten thousand minus the three thousand two hundred means there's actually a cost in dollars of six thousand eight hundred.

But what's it in terms of a percent then? In terms of a percent, we would just say, well then let's just take that cost of the debt after taxes, the six thousand eight hundred, and compare it to the debt itself, the one hundred thousand six eight divided by one hundred is going to give us then that six point eight again, six point eight. This is worth doing. I think it's easier. It gives you more information or it's more intuitive, although longer. You want to memorize the formula, however, for tax, for practice problems and just make things easier. Let's do that same thing, the same calculation. I'm going to try to get to this number now that the six thousand eight, but use our quick formula in order to get there.

So if we say the debt is going to be that one hundred thousand one hundred thousand debt, we'll just instead of doing that two step method, I'm just going to say let's just multiply times the cost, the debt, after tax percent, which is the formula of 10 percent times one minus the tax rate or one hundred percent minus the tax rate. Right. One minus the point one, you know, it would be one hundred percent minus thirty two percent or one minus point three two. However you want to think about it multiplying ten times to the point six, eight then gives us the six point eight and then I can get directly to the six thousand eight hundred instead of using a two step method by simply taking the one hundred thousand times these six point eight, this is going to be a little bit cleaner to use something like this.

Possibly if I'm comparing multiple different options and trying to present multiple different options and analyze them and think about them and see what we want to do. So let's do it again here. Let's do it again, because this is fun. So next time now we've got eight percent on the rate and now the tax rate is 40 percent. We won't think about the debt first. We're just going to think about our formula. The thing you want to memorize here that's going to then be the interest rate is the eight percent. Then we have the one multiplied times, one minus the tax rate, one or one hundred percent. This time we showed it as a percent, one hundred percent instead of one one hundred percent minus the 40 percent.

Or you could say one minus point four is going to give us the sixty percent, 60 percent times eight means that after taxes we got the four point eight percent actual cost of the financing. Even though we're paying eight percent, we're getting the tax benefit, therefore four point eight. That means when we compare it to other options that don't have a tax impact, equity options, for example, possibly then we possibly want to use the four point eight to be fair, between the options and then down below, we've got the one hundred thousand. Let's figure, let's just try to do this intuitively and say, well, let's pull in the debt of one hundred thousand and then recalculate what the actual cost would be in terms of dollars and in terms of percent. Let's do that.

So we have the interest, the debt's going to be the one hundred thousand interest rate, eight percent we're going to be paying then the eight thousand dollars. It's going to cost the state thousands. But we get a tax benefit for taking on the debt because that interest is deductible. Tax benefit is going to be at eight thousand. That's going to be deducted because it's on the income statement and we have an income tax and lowers the income taxable income, which lowers the amount of tax we pay. And we're going to say it's at the margin, which is a 40 percent tax and 40 percent. So we're going to say then the eight thousand times forty percent, that means there's a tax benefit of three thousand two hundred. So the eight thousand minus the three thousand two hundred that we kind of get back or we get to reduce our taxes by means, there's a net cost of four thousand eight hundred. So that's the net cost in dollars.

But now let's compare that to the debt to figure out the. Percentage, I want to know what the percentage cost would be, so then we take that four thousand eight hundred divided by one hundred thousand dollar debt, and that would then give us the four point eight percent again so we could do that one a little bit more quickly. Now, let's try to get to this number, the four thousand eight hundred, by using our quick kind of calculation of the actual cost after after taxes, percent calculation. So now we're then going to take the debt, the one hundred thousand pick up our cost of debt after taxes. This is the part where you want to memorize the formula.

You want to know if interest rates are going to be the eight percent minus one minus the tax rate, which is one minus the rate of point four or forty percent or one hundred percent minus 40 percent. Eight times the sixty or eight percent times the 60 percent is going to give us the four point eight, then I can go directly to the end result here, taking that one hundred thousand times to four point eight instead of taking the two step method, we kind of did up top to get to the dollar amount of the cost of the four thousand eight hundred.

Cost of Debt After Tax Interest Rate Calculation

Closing up the icon. We have our information up top and will go through the calculations down below. We're looking into the debt financing again, noticing that as we think about these, you're keeping in the back of your mind the financing of the company, how to get money to finance the company could either be done in the form of debt or equity, focusing on debt here. When we think about debt, we have to take into consideration tax consequences, which can complicate things a bit because of it. So now we have the cost after tax, we're going to say is the 10 percent. So we're given the cost after taxes.

It's probably a situation in practice that would be a little bit more unusual because normally you would have the cost or basically the interest rate in practice and figuring out the cost after taxes. This is something that helps you understand the problem more and is typically something you'll see in a book type of problem to test whether or not you understand the problem more. And so then we have the tax rate going to be the thirty five percent remembering that we're typically taking one rate, even though we have a progressive tax system, possibly not the average rate because we make our decisions on the margin. The last decision being at the last rate, possibly being our highest tax rate than you think? Possibly.

So what is the debt rate, the example debt? We have one hundred thousand. So we'll do this once again without basically thinking about a debt amount and we're just thinking about the percentages without even the need to know what basically the debt is. Then we'll take into consideration the debt and think of it as an example to get it better in our minds. Now, in a prior chapter, we did this kind of the standard way in the formula that you want to have in your mind is the cost of debt after taxes, which would be the debt rate. It's going to equal the debt rate normally, like the interest rate, the rent on the money, the cost of the debt, the cost of borrowing, the cost of having the use of the money, kind of like rent, but interest typically times one minus the tax rate. That's going to be our formula.

Now, if you plug this in algebraically, then here the thing we're looking for is the debt rate, or kind of like the interest rate, which again, a little bit unusual, but it's just an algebraic equation. So if we have one unknown and we have all the others known, we could plug it into our algebraic equation and find the unknown. So the cost of debt after tax is given at the 10 percent that would be the 10 percent equals the debt rate. That's the unknown. We don't know that one. That's why we call it unknown times one minus the tax rate, which we do know the tax rate. It's the thirty five percent then you could solve using your algebra for the unknown and figure it that way. We'll also do it with the tables down here.

Just put it in the normal table that we saw in the past. I'm not going to rework it to calculate the debt rate first and then we'll rework it, basically doing the algebra in the second calculation. So what we had last time is the same problem, the same format in our table, which would be the interest rate, and then I'll bring it into the inside one minus the tax rate. So the interest rate is what we would not know. I put the answer here, but it's yellow just to indicate that that would be basically the unknown at this point in time. And then we got one minus the tax rate. So we got one hundred percent or one minus the tax rate, which is thirty five percent or point three five, the difference being sixty five percent. And so then we know the end result is the 10 percent.

So 10 percent is the end result as we can see here. Normally then we would be taking the fifteen point three, eight times the sixty five. If I do this backwards, basically now I know the 10 percent, I know the sixty five. In this case I'm trying to get back to fifteen percent. Then we would be fifteen point three eight percent. We would be taking point one divided by the point sixty five. And that's going to give us our point one five three eight and so on or fifteen point three eight percent. You can then double check it by taking this number one five three eight times the point sixty five, getting back down to the 10 percent or zero point one. If we were to rework the algebra then you can do that this way. So just note that if you memorize something,

Tables, if you like to visualize things and tables, many people, obviously, if you work with book problems, will like writing it out algebraically because you've been doing a lot of math in schools and whatnot. Right. But the more people use tables and start using Excel, which will be highly effective to do, you'll start seeing things possibly in tables. That's not not really a bad thing. Oftentimes you don't need to rework the table to basically back into the number up top. If you think of things this way, you can even list it out this way. If you're writing it down, if that's clearer in your mind, you could do that. Then if we take the algebra here and we reform it, basically solving for the debt rate, our table would look something like this. And if you look at a typical kind of answer key to a kind of problem you see like this in a book, it would rework it to basically this formula. This would be all you would see.

Just remember, any time you see that, you start to think, well, do I have to memorize another formula? And you've got to know, like know what you do if you're just using the algebra in this format. You want to be able to recognize that you can plug this into this formula with the one unknown, then solve for it if you then reworked it to get to the bottom line being the debt rate would look something like this. We've got the cost of debt after taxes. Then we'll pull in the one minus the tax rate, which is once again the one hundred percent minus the thirty five percent, the tax rate one minus the thirty five percent or one minus point thirty five or one hundred percent, minus thirty five percent. That gives us then sixty five percent.

And then we have again the point one point one or 10 percent divided by the point six five. That gives us the point one five three eight four or the fifteen point three eight percent about. Then if we plug this it's often useful to plug this into a table. I won't rework it this way. You could use like a goal, seek to kind of rework it in this format if you would like to as well. But I'm just going to plug it back into the table so it can kind of make sense on what this actually means. So let's imagine we have a debt amount of one hundred thousand and just work out these calculations. Let's say we have the interest going to be the debt times, the interest which we have now found.

That's going to be the fifteen point three eight percent that's going to be like the interest rate that we have. That means that the interest payments that we would have would be the 15th, three eighty five about rounded. And then we have a tax benefit related to this. To the tax benefit would then be the deduction of the interest, the fifteen three, eighty five and thirty five percent of that we would get a tax benefit for. So now we've got fifteen three, eighty five times the point thirty five or thirty five percent giving us a tax benefit of five thousand three eighty five. Therefore we would have fifteen three eighty five interest expenses. The rent on the money interest minus the five thousand three eighty five means that we have the ten thousand cost of debt after taxes. So there's the cost of debt after taxes. What would be the rate then based on this? Let's get to the rate.

We're going to say the cost of debt after taxes would be this number, the ten thousand divided by or compared to the original debt, the one hundred thousand, which would then give us our 10 percent dividing out the ten thousand divided by the one hundred thousand gives us basically our 10 percent. Oftentimes it's worthwhile with these kinds of problems to kind of work in an actual no amount and work this out in this format, which is the way that you would probably be most intuitive to think about. Just to reiterate what is actually going on when you're thinking about things, just in terms of percents in general, very useful to work these out in Excel, highly recommend doing that. Obviously, if you're working on test questions and you see things in an algebraic format as opposed to a table format, then it's worthwhile to pull out the old paper and pencil, get ready for the format that you will see this in a test situation, do the algebra, write it down in that way as well.

Cost of Debt After Tax Interest Rate Calculation

We have our information up top. We will then go through the calculations for it down below. Keeping in mind in the back of your mind in the chapter that we're looking at financing type of issues, when you're thinking about financing type of issues, getting money, getting capital for the operation of the organization, you have two categories, two main categories, that being debt, that being equity. We're focusing here on debt. When you're dealing with debt, you also have to be dealing with the tax consequences because you have interest typically, which will have a tax consequence due to it being an income statement type of thing and the tax being an income tax. And so now we're going to be looking at the bond type of situation.

So when you're looking at bonds, also note you have the added level of complication in that there's going to be a rate on the bond and there's also going to be a kind of a market rate or yield to maturity type of rate. And so your question is, well, which one am I going to use with my calculations here? And the answer typically will be the market rate will discuss kind of why that would be. It might not sound as intuitive as to why it would be because you might be saying, hey, look, I mean, it seems like I'm actually paying the interest on the interest rate, on the bond. And so why would it be like the market rate? But the difference between the discount and the premium is something that we basically are going to amortize and in essence, expense in some way typically. And therefore, that's really kind of a true market rate.

That's so that's what we'll use so that hopefully that will become a little bit more clear. But just in terms of practice, you just kind of want to memorize that of the two if you're basically using market rate. So we have the poor value we're saying is the one thousand we have a year to maturity or we're going to say twenty five. The annual interest payment, we're going to say is 90. That means that the interest rate on the bond is ninety, divided by one thousand or nine percent. So nine percent bond interest rate. And then the current market price is 930 tax rate. Thirty five percent. So what they did not give us here, they did not give us the rate, the market rate, but instead gave us the price of the nine 930 if they had given us the market rate. It's a fairly straightforward problem because then we could just take that market rate. The question then would simply be, do we take the market rate or do we take the rate on the bond? The rate on the bond, in essence, 90 divided by one thousand nine percent market rate is whatever it will be.

We'll have to figure it out now. But if we had that, then we would choose the market rate in order to do our calculation and then do a similar calculation that we have seen in our prior debt kind of problems. So here we got that added step of trying to find the market rate based on the current market price. A little added bit of difficulty. This first step, however, something that we did basically in the prior chapter when we talked about just bonds in general. So we have to do that first and then do the new thing, which will be fairly straightforward as long as we pick up the proper rate, which will be the market rate, which is the one we're thinking of finding here.

OK, so first I'm going to think about how we can do this first part, just basically find the market rate using Gosuke because it's a little bit more complicated of a problem than you would think. And again, you can look at the prior chapters in the prior chapter to get more information on this. So I go a little bit faster on it. But first, we kind of want to think about our normal calculation. If we had the market rate and then try to back it and what we should do to back into it, normally we would do a present value of an annuity and then present value of one for the series of interest payments, the annuity for the payment at maturity, present value of one using the rate, the market rate, and then we would add them up to get to the total.

Now it's a little bit difficult to come up with an algebraic equation then, because these two components were basically adding together two to two formulas here to find the unknown. So you could do it. But it gets a little bit long to do. And so therefore it's really useful to use something like Excel in order to do this type of calculation. There's two ways that you can do that. You could do that one using the same calculation and then using a gold stick. And two, you can use the rate function. However, even if using the rate function, you'd still probably want to check your answer with the present value of annuity and present value of one calculation, so let's do it the first way, because I think this is actually a little bit more intuitive way to do it.

We do this in Excel as well, if you want to see all the steps within Excel to do this too. So let's imagine that we have the goal secure. And what we would first do is come up with some rate. We're going to imagine a rate. So this happens to be the answer. But when we first start, we could just put five percent or whatever here to start with so that we have something to fill out our function with because the cell is geared to or included in both these two calculations as well as this totaling up these two cells, then we can then ask IXL to change this number, say, hey, Excel, would you change this number to see what it should be in order to get this number, to know what it needs to be? That being the 930 and we can basically do that in Excel, we'll do that basically automatically and allow us to do that. So if we would do the present value of an annuity, it would be a negative present value.

The rate then would be we're assuming this rate, which when we started off, would be something that possibly we don't know what it is yet. We would just use that cell with something in it, comma number of periods, which would be the 25 periods, comma, and then the payment was given at the 90, which means a nine percent rate because it would be the one thousand times nine percent would be the 90 that would then give us the present value of the annuity eight thirty to forty five. Then we'd get the present value of one, which is the one thousand at the end of the maturity date that would be present value of the rate, which once again would be the this rate that we would be using up top number of periods, number of periods would be twenty five and then we would not have a payment this time and instead have the future value go down here this time, which would be the one thousand dollars that would give us the ninety seven fifty five.

Adding these two sales up would get us to the price. Now if we just guessed what this number should be, the price would not match what we think it should match, which is that nine 930. And we could basically ask Excel to then change the cell just basically with brute force until we get the sale to be what it should be, using a tool called Goal Seek. It can basically do that in that format. Then we can kind of use this whole kind of function as if it's an algebraic equation, as if we're solving for the one unknown without reworking it to solve for that unknown. Right. We could just basically use Gorsky to find it through trial and error. And that's one method. I think that's one of the more intuitive methods. There's also a function in Excel to solve for the rate, but it's a little bit more complicated of a function.

And again, you get there nice and quickly and easily if you plug in the information correctly. But once done, you probably still want to check it by using that rate to then calculate your present value of the annuity present value of one and see if you do indeed get back to the number that you think you should have in the nine. So this formula would be equal to the rate brackets and then the number of periods, which is going to be the twenty five comma, the payment, the payment that is going to be the ninety, which would be the nine percent of the one thousand comma the present value note here, you got to put a negative here or else it will not calculate properly. So it's got to be a negative present value. That's going to be the price now that 930 which this is known to us, comma, and then we've got the future value, the future.

Hold on a sec. The number of the present value is going to be the nine thirty and then the future value, which is going to be the one thousand, the one thousand up top. So let me see if I can get these correct. Again, the thing that has a negative in it is the payment amount, the payment of the ninety and then the future value of the one thousand. Those are the things that need to be negative, the number of periods and then the present value, not negative. If you do that properly, you'll get to that nine point seventy six. And then once you have that, I would then double check it with your normal calculations.

Once you have the market value to calculate the present value of annuity, the present value of one double checking that you do indeed get down to that nine thirty. OK, so. So now that we have that, then we can do our normal kind of calculation to take into consideration the tax impact so we could do our cost of debt after tax kind of calculation. We're just going to do a similar thing that we did in a prior chapter. Now we've got the interest rate, this being the market rate. That's been the main question or the new thing from the prior about looking into bonds. That's going to be the nine point six seven as opposed to the bond rate, which would be nine percent ninety divided by one thousand. Then we've got the one plus one minus the tax rate or one hundred percent or one minus the tax rate, which was said to be thirty five percent. So one minus point three.

Five or one hundred percent, minus 35 percent, that will give us the sixty five percent, remembering the logic here, we're basically saying, you know, this is the change that could be happening to net income that is going to have a tax impact of that change. We got the thirty five percent, which we're basically going to get back in taxes. We're going have to pay the interest on it and kind of get it back in taxes to some degree. So therefore, the amount not impacted or that we're not going to get back is going to be sixty five percent. So if I take that sixty five percent times the nine point sixty five, that's going to have a cost of debt at the six point three four. So we're saying, OK, for the bond that is issued, we have a couple of rates.

We've got the nine percent rate on the bond, which is the actual interest rate that we're paying. But when we think about the cost of debt, we're really thinking about the market rate, the nine point seventy six. Now, why does that make sense? Why is that the market rate? Because we're going to actually expense the actual money that we're going to pay. Right. So how does that make sense? Well, the difference between the 930 and the one thousand in this case being a discount, if it was going the other way, it would be a premium that is different. That difference is something that's going to kind of be from an accounting standpoint, we're going to have to basically amortize it over the life of this thing, either straight line or using an effective type of method.

And therefore, you know, the real difference is going to have an impact on the income statement over the life of the bond. And therefore, on average, we can kind of use the market rate. Their market rate is actually basically the cost that we're using, even though we're paying interest rate at the rate on the bond. So we're using the market rate, which is kind of appropriate, and then we're adjusting for taxes basically like an average kind of annual basis being the six point three four. So there we have that. Now, if I was to put that into our example, just to calculate this out, to look something like this, we have the interest market rate. If we have a debt of one thousand times the interest that we had, remember, we just calculated the interest up to seventy six nine points.

That would be once again the market rate. That's not the actual interest we pay. But that's kind of the interest when you take into consideration the payment price that we receive, the difference either the premium or discount, in this case the discount. And so we've got the one thousand times the nine point seventy six percent is ninety seven point five seven taken then into consideration the tax benefit. We have the interest, expense or deduction, the ninety seven point five, seven times the tax rate, the thirty five percent. That's going to give us thirty four points, one five. If we take then the ninety seven point five seven minus the thirty four point one five weeks and then the cost of debt after taxes, the sixty three point four to and that's in dollars.

If we then take the cost of debt after tax percent, we're going to take that amount divided by the original debt as half the one thousand that would then give us our six point three four, which is Of course our six point three four up top. Confusing thing about this, again, is the fact that you're looking at this rate and you're saying, well, wait, that's not I mean, that rate isn't the rate that we're actually paying the interest on. But you've got to consider the fact that the difference between, in this case, the discount and the amount of the bond is basically interest and will have a tax impact over the life of the bond. You would think, given the fact that we're going to amortize that in some way over our life, that difference then has an impact on the income statement as we do so. OK, so let's go back down and let's do this again, this time with a premium.

So the par value now is one thousand the year to maturity. Twenty five, the annual interest rate, now 90. The current market price is now one thousand one fifteen. So now it's at a premium tax rate of thirty five. So the difficult part is to find the market rate first because they didn't give it to us. This is the part of the problem that's really in the bond, kind of in the last area that we looked at, where we focused specifically on bonds. And now we've got to find that first so that we can use the proper rate, which once again is the market rate, as opposed to the rate on the bond. So if we use the goal, seek to do that, we could say, OK, we'll just plug something into the rate calculation and then do our calculations, as we normally would if we knew the rate.

And we're looking for the total price, the total price being known to us given here, then we'll use a goal, seek to change this amount to whatever it needs to be to get to the number that needs to be at. And that's kind of like using algebra without reworking that same kind of algebraic concept. We only have one unknown within this whole set of series of things. But instead of reworking everything to solve for that unknown, we'll use brute force trial and error. So we've got the present value of the annuity, which would be the present value of the rate, the rate then is this amount that which is going to make up first and then we would change it to what it needs to be a number of periods, which is going to be the twenty five comma the payment, which is going to be 90 on the payment.

And that will then give us our present value of the annuity. Ninety six point five seven present value of one present value of the one thousand at maturity would then be the present value of the rate. The rate is going to be this amount up top again, comma number of periods, which is going to be twenty five and then not a payment, but rather the future value because its present value of one that one thousand. That then gives us the one forty eight forty three adding the annuity and the present value of one gives us the total. If this had not been, if we didn't have the answer up here, if this was something other than the percent being used like five percent, we can then ask Excel, would you please change this cell to whatever it needs to be, just using trial and error, using brute force to get to this end number to be what we know it should be, because it's part of our dataset so we can then solve for the unknown in that way.

Now, you can also use another formula called the rate formula to do this, even if you use the rate formula. However, once you get the number, you still probably want to double check it with the present value of annuity and present value of one rate formula. Looks like this equals the rate brackets number of periods, which is going to be twenty five comma. You need a negative number here. The payment which is going to be 90 comma future value, the future value, the present, the present value is going to be the one one one five the price comma future value. You need a negative here and this is going to be then the one thousand that will be there at maturity that should give you the nine point nine seven nine three, which you can then double check with your annuity calculations.

Also note that when you use this method and any other method you use, you should have kind of an idea of what you expect the rate to be. Because I know the rate up top is ninety, divided by ten, divided by one thousand, which is nine percent. So I know what the rate is for the rate on the bond. They're issued at a premium. So if they're issued at a premium, that means that basically the rate on the bond has to be higher than the rate on the market because the people on the market can't get a can't get any other investment that's similar at the same rate. Therefore, they're willing to pay a premium. So you would expect this number to be lower than in our case, nine percent. If it's not, then that's an indication that either you're thinking something wrong and you got to mull it over a bit to get it figured out so then we can plug into our cost of debt calculation. So the interest rate is now seven point nine three. Big point here.

We're using the seven point nine three market rate as opposed to the ninety divided by one thousand bond rate. And once we have that, then we have our same calculation we saw in our prior problems for debt, one minus the tax rate or one hundred percent, minus the thirty five percent, which is the tax rate. You can also think about it as one minus the point three five. That gives us the sixty five percent, sixty five percent or point six five times seven point nine three or point seven nine three gives us the five point one five. So this then being the rate five point one five percent that we think of as the cost of the debt as opposed to the seven point nine three. Again, if you look at this a little confusing because you got three rates, your rate on the bond is ninety divided by one thousand, the rate we actually pay.

But we issued at a premium, we issued at a premium because the market rate, in essence, is different. That means that when we record it, we're going to have to basically amortize the premium over the life of the bond. So it will have an impact on the income statement and therefore a tax impact as well. And so the actual rate basically kind of like an average rate in general over the life we're thinking is going to be this five point one five percent. Now, if you plug this into like our example, just to calculate this out, to make sense, to kind of make sense of it, you'd say, OK, the interest is going to be one thousand times the interest rate, which is the market rate.

Again, this is a little tricky because this rate is basically the market rate, not the rate we're actually paying. But you can get an idea of what the interest expense will be over the life due to this, because you're going to have to be amortizing the premium. And that's why that's why it kind of makes sense. So we've got the one thousand times the seven point nine three is the seventy nine point two nine. Then we can look at the tax benefit. That would be the interest expense, which we're assuming to be seventy nine point seventy nine in general times the tax rate of point thirty five tax benefit, twenty seven point seventy five. Therefore, the. Seventy nine point two nine minus to twenty seven point seventy five gives us the fifty one point five for cost of debt after taxes in dollars, then we can calculate the percent cost, which would be the cost of debt after taxes in dollars fifty one point fifty four divided by the debt, which is the one thousand given us then that five point one five percent.

Calculate Change in Cost of Debt After tax Due to Reduced Tax

We have our information on the left hand side. We'll use the calculator on the right hand side. Remember, as we're going through these practice problems, we're focusing on the financing of the companies you're keeping in the back of your mind. The idea that you want the money to finance operations of the organization which we can get, and two major categories or classes, one, debt financing to equity financing. When we focus on the debt financing as we are here, we need to take into account the added consideration of the tax impact, especially if we're going to try to compare different financing options to, say, equity items which do not have that tax impact related to them. So we're going to have the cost outstanding. We have a bond.

We're going to have a bond or issue in the bond, and then we're going to imagine a situation where circumstances have changed and see what the difference would be if we issued the bond at a different time in the future. So we have the bond outstanding, we're going to say it is nine percent, nine percent on the bond. We imagine that being the rate on the bond yield to maturity or the market rate that demanded rate of return yield to maturity, 12 percent that not on the bond, the tax rate is going to be the. Thirty five percent, remember? And when we think about the tax rate, we might be thinking about the tax rate on the margin, even though we have a progressive tax system, therefore taking basically the highest tax rate, because that's where we're kind of at at this point in time.

When we make a new decision, then we have the after tax cost of debt. That's what we're basically going to be looking at. And we're going to assume the par value. Once we do the calculation with just basically percentages, then we'll do another calculation with the par value so that we can basically think this through with actual dollar amounts. Then we'll do another one saying, well, what if the tax rate changes to twenty five percent? And what if there then is a change in the market for the yield to maturity to change to 10 percent? What would then be the impact or the cost of debt at that point in time if we were to take out new debt at that point in time? So it's going to be a great problem. Here we go. The cost of debt after taxes, we're going to be considering it first on a percentage basis, straightforward, like the other cost of debt type of calculations.

The only thing different with the bond is that we're considering the interest rate, not the rate on the bond, but the market rate. You got to pick up the market rate. That could be a little bit confusing because you're probably thinking, hey, look, when I pay the annual interest on pain at the rate of nine percent, why am I picking up the 12 percent? And once again, kind of like the average buffer between all the payments is going to be the 12 percent. Because in this case, given the fact that the rate on the bond is less than the rate on the market, you would expect that we issue the bond at a discount at that point in time because the people that can get basically a better rate elsewhere. So for us to sell our bond, we would have to sell it at a discount. That difference between the discount and the par value is basically due to interest.

And from an accounting standpoint, we would actually then expense that interest over time. So it could have been a tax impact. So it still is something. So on average, you can kind of think of it as the market rate, as being the actual kind of rate. That is the cost. Given those components and there will be a tax impact for it, then we're going to take the one minus the tax rate. So one hundred percent or one one or one hundred percent minus the tax rate, which would be point twenty five or thirty five percent. And that's going to give us then the sixty five percent or the point sixty five. Then we take the twelve and multiply it times the point sixty five to get the seven point eight. So remember point one, two or twelve percent times the point six five. It's going to give us the zero point zero seven eight. Otherwise No.

One, if we move the decimal over seven point eight percent. So that would be the cost. And we can kind of compare that then to other types of financing options and get some kind of good, good estimates between them as we take into account the taxes that will be impacted. Note, though, as we do that, that bonds, Of course, do have an expiration date and whatnot. So it's still kind of a little bit difficult to think about the different options between. And debt, but that's going to be our idea here. Now, if we actually add in the one thousand dollars and try to calculate this out, this makes more intuitive sense oftentimes to people to say, hey, the percent makes sense. Kind of. But let me put in some numbers here and calculate it again with an example.

Look, something like this interest calculation would be the thousand times the 12 percent goes to multiply that times to 12 percent, which is the market rate. Once again, you're going to say, hey, but I'm not really paying 12 percent and I'm paying nine percent. That's how much interest is going out. But as we amortize the discount or premium, whichever the case would would be, we have to basically, you know, we will have an impact of the difference and which is a result of a difference between the price and and the poor value or the amount that we're going to pay at maturity. So that's why on average, we're kind of using that 12 percent, even though it's a bond here.

So the one thousand times to 12 percent means the interest would be on average, that one hundred and twenty, the one hundred and twenty per year. And then we have the tax benefit of that would be the interest deduction, because now this would be good for taxes of one 20 times the tax rate or thirty five percent, one twenty times thirty five means basically of this one twenty. And we're going to have to in essence pay. We're going to get it back in terms of taxes of like forty two. So one twenty minus forty two is seventy eight cost of debt after the tax impact then if we want to get back to the percent cost we could say, well then let's take that 78 percent and compare it to the debt, the one thousand and that then seventy eight divided by one thousand would give us that seven point eight percent, seven point eight percent that we got in this format up top as well.

So obviously you want to kind of understand this formula, basically, which is the market rate or the rate of of the debt, which in this case, if it's a bond market rate times one minus the tax rate, you want to understand that you can go to do a nice quick calculation, often useful, however, to then work out the example and calculate it in this format, useful for your own understanding and often useful to to basically show someone else's understanding of it as well. So then we could say, well, what would happen then if there is a change and now there is a tax rate change to twenty five percent. So that's good. So we look better there. And then the rate, the change in the yield, meaning the market rate on the bonds, is now 10 percent, even though the bond we're still saying has a rate of nine percent on the actual bond.

So then let's do the calculation. I'm not sure if we were to do financing again in this time period. So now we're going to say what would financing cost at this time? Also note that when we're actually generating the bond, if we're generating a new bond, we might try to match the market rate here, which would be, you know, in this case, the 10 percent as we generate the bond, once the bonds generated, Of course, then the rate on the bond will differ after some time passes to the market rate. But for book problem purposes, we want to basically make sure that we understand when we're trying to present value, when we're trying to see the cost, we're picking up the proper rate, which typically will not be the rate on the bond, but the market rate.

And due to the reasons we basically talked about, that's kind of the tricky thing with the bond side of the debt financing. OK, so if we know that, then we're going to say, all right, well, then we'll just take the interest rate, which is now 10 percent. If we wanted to issue it, finance with some bonds here. And then we're going to take the tax impact one minus the tax rate, one hundred percent or one minus the tax rate, point twenty five or twenty five percent. That gives us 100 percent minus twenty five percent. Seventy five. And then we take 10 percent times the seventy five. That gives us the seven point five percent. Remember, this calculation right here might make some sense to kind of mull it over in your mind. It'll be easier to remember this one hundred percent. You can kind of think of the change in the net income, the taxable income, which is going to be taxed, and then twenty five of it, you're kind of getting back.

Therefore, the seventy five percent of it will be the actual impact times the rate, which is the 10 percent that's giving us that seven point five percent. Therefore seven point five percent is the cost we're thinking after taxes as opposed to the 10 percent. So if we were to compare this to something else that doesn't have a similar tax impact, such as not debt financing, but rather equity financing, then we could try to compare something that's more matchable apples to apples, as they say. Same thing to the same thing is what that means. So now we're going to go to the example down here and let's just plug in our one thousand dollar par value and just work this out again and look at it this way. The debt would be one thousand, we're going to say.

And that's what we would get because we're issuing the one thousand. We're going to receive one thousand. We are imagining the cost is going to be 10 percent. In terms of interest. We're not actually. 10 percent, we're going to imagine we're paying the nine percent here, but using the market rate because of the fact that we would have to issue this time, this time the rate on the market is 10 percent. It's still higher than the rate on the bond. And therefore, we'd still have a discount and we'd have to then account for that. That discount that we give versus the maturity date is due to the difference in rates. So we'll amortize the discounts and we'll have a tax impact of it and so on. So that's why we're using the market rate.

So one thousand times the 10 percent, one hundred dollars tax impact on average for the life of the bond here, which does have a maturity date, which is a little different than possibly equity kind of methods here. But we've got the one thousand times the twenty one hundred times the twenty five percent, because this interest deduction is like a deduction and tax rate. Twenty five percent. So one hundred dollars times twenty five tax benefits of twenty five or so of the hundred dollars that we're going to have to pay basically on average over the life of the bond here, we're going to get back in terms of tax benefits. Twenty five dollars. So the net impact being seventy five cost debt after the taxes in terms of dollars.

But we want the percent because then we can use the percent to calculate. So we can then just say let's take that cost of debt after taxes to seventy five, compare it to the original debt. What we got, which is in this case one thousand seventy five divided by one thousand is seven point five seven point five. Same calculation. Then we got up to the seven point five now on a percentage basis taking into consideration the tax impact, something that could be more plausible, easier for us, better decision making process if we compare it to something that doesn't have the tax impact. Just note, by the way, if we're comparing, obviously, debt to debt kind of calculations, it's not quite as important, Of course, because both of those have a similar kind of tax impact. So it might be worth doing in that case. But again, if you're comparing to other types of financing that don't have that same tax impact, such as equity financing, that's when it becomes a little bit more difficult for us to do those kinds of comparisons between different types of financing. We're looking for ways to make that comparison, to make that decision easier.

Cost of Preferred Stock Percent

Remember that we are talking about the financing of the organization. Two main categories to keep in mind. We've been looking in prior chapters at the debt category. When thinking about the debt category, you've got to take into consideration the tax impact versus the equity category when taken into the equity category. We do not have that same kind of tax impact, but we do have that added complication of the equity kind of side of things. When we're on equity. Common stock is usually the thing that we would think about, meaning the ownership of the organization, given an equity interest in the organization with voting rights and whatnot with it. However, we also have the preferred stock, which is a bit more limited and thereby being a little bit easier for us to calculate typically due to that.

So that's what we'll go to first here on the equity side, and then we'll move on to the common stock in future chapters. So we can sell the preferred stock, we're saying at the 150 and the estimated flotation costs, which we're going to say are the costs of us in order to issue the preferred stock. When you think of flotation costs, you can think about the cost of floating the stock out there to see if you can sell it, float it out on the market. You know, those are going to be the costs for us to get these stocks out there one time costs as opposed to the dividends. Dividends are going to be the things that are going to be the annual cost that we're going to basically have to pay.

The preferred stock, you'll recall, is a little bit more standardized in terms of the dividends that we are believing that we're going to be issuing when we move to the common stocks, the dividends can be a little bit more confusing, and we typically have to take into consideration the value of the stock a little bit more closely, given the fact that we're giving kind of an equity interest, voting rights in it and that type of situation. Also note, when you're considering this, we're going to be trying to compare this percent to something like debt financing. Debt financing has a maturity date. So you've got to keep that in mind as you do these calculations. You know, when you think about a bond, it might be like a 30 year bond or something like that, but it still ends in 30 years.

When you're thinking about the shares, then it doesn't really have that same kind of term termination date. It's just we're going to assume dividends of nine dollars annually as basically the cost that we're going to try to compare on a percentage basis. So we'll do the same kind of percentage calculation here so we can compare, as they say, apples to apples to other financing methods, possibly including debt financing methods. So we have the annual dividends per share, we're going to say nine dollars. That's what's going to cost us. It's going to cost us that on an annual basis in order to get one hundred and fifty dollars, because that's what we're going to sell it for per share. But we're not actually going to get one 50 because there's a one time cost.

So that's why I'm going to have a subcategory of the net sales price, I'm going to call it, which is the sales price of that one fifty minus the flotation cost. These two costs are not the same and that the nine dollar cost is what we think we're going to have to pay on an annual basis. We're at the flotation costs. Are the costs for us to get the money out there right now. So in order to get the one 150, we're not actually going to get one fifty after we basically make the sale, because although that's the price we have to pay out the four dollars at that same point in time, basically, and we're actually going to get the one forty six. So in order to get the 146 dollars, we're going to have to then pay on an annual basis.

We're saying a dividend of nine percent once we have that of the nine dollars, not nine percent. Once we have that, we could take the nine dollars divided by the 146 and that will then give us our rate here. And that's going to be if we move the decimal over the six point one six about. So once we take into consideration any flotation, which can complicate things a little bit, it's a pretty straightforward calculation for us to get a cost of preferred stock percent that we can then kind of compare out and then note what we do not have here in this calculation. We do not have the added complication of the tax impact because this is an equity. Situation when we pay out the dividends, in other words, it's not impacting the income statement because we're taking it out of equity on the balance sheet.

And so it doesn't have that that tax effect, as does the the debt financing, which typically the the payment that we have to pay out is in the form of interest, which is an expense on the income statement, thereby having an impact typically on taxable income, net income, taxable income, and therefore having a tax implication as well. Then when we move on to the common stocks, then we have to add an added level of complexity in that we think of the common stocks as basically having a claim to the net value of the company. So we then have to think about the growth kind of component, and we also might have to think more in depth about the change and the dividends that could be taking place.

So we have to consider those options as well. When we move on to the other side of equity, which would be the common stock, probably the more common thought when we're thinking about the equity side of things, people have an equity interest in ownership interest. And in that format, you know, you're thinking about the accounting equation formatted as assets minus liabilities equals the equity or the net asset type of calculation. And the value of that is something that would be given as well in terms of issuing the common stock.

Financing Common Stock Prob 1

Our information is up top. We'll do the calculations then down below for them. Remember, we're keeping our mind in on financing of the company. How can we finance the company? Two main categories. We have the debt financing, which we've talked about in prior chapters and the equity financing where we are focusing now. When we think about the debt financing, we have to deal with the fact that the major thing we have to pay for is going to be interest on the debt. Interest is going to be taxable on the income statements, on the income statement, and therefore taxable and deductible possibly for taxes. And therefore, we have to counterbalance the tax impact as well as the cost of the financing.

If we want to compare it to something like financing with equity, where we do not have that issue with the tax impact, the major equity thing that we would be thinking of is the common stock. That's the first thing that would come to mind. Typically when we're thinking about financing through equity, basically giving some other people the shares shares, giving them access basically to the company as an ownership interest in the company REITs, then possibly to the earnings of the company to be distributed in the form of dividends, as is going to be declared by the company, the the dividend policy of the company. And so and also had voting rights within the company as well. So we're issuing the common stock.

Also note, there's some differences between the bonds and the stocks in that if you're looking at bonds or some kind of debt financing, there's typically going to be some type of maturity date. When you're thinking about the common stock, then you don't really have that in the basic data. You're going to have a similar kind of payments that could happen from the company, which in this case would be the dividends that would be going out as opposed to the interest payments when you're thinking about something like debt. But we also have to consider that there's equity financing within the company. And so you can think about it. Of course, if we think of the common stockholders as we do as owners of the company, the owners have the equity claim to the company.

So from an accounting standpoint, if you rework the accounting equation as assets minus liabilities equals equity, then that kind of equity component or the net value assets minus liabilities equal. The net value of the company is part of what is owned, in essence by the common stockholders. You can basically think of it that way as well. Therefore, we have to not only account for the dividends, which would kind of be like the cash flow impact, but also for the value of the stock. And we're assuming that it's going to go up or the value of the company increases and thereby the value of the stock, the equity interest increases in a similar way. So it's a bit more confusing. And that way, note also the dividends could vary.

They could change from year to year. So that could be a little bit more difficult than, say, the preferred stock where you don't have the same kind of thought process that you have. The ownership of the company and the dividends are typically a bit more fixed there. So let's look at the information. We got the dividends per share, two dollars. We have the common stock price. This is what we're assuming we can sell it for. We will sell it on the market. So we're going to sell it for whatever we can get for it. But remember, this is a sale that's coming directly from the company. The proceeds then go to the company in this case, rather than a trade for stocks that are already on the market, the expected growth is going to be twelve percent. And then we're going to say there's a floatation cost of four dollars.

So we'll do this calculation a couple different ways. The first way we're going to call the cost of retained earnings, which we're going to say is the dividends divided by the common stock price that we're going to issue. We're going to do this first in the order of operations and then add the growth rate to get the total cost. So let's see what that looks like. If we put that into a table type of format, we're going to say in order to get the money, the money is going to be forty dollars per share. So in order to get that, we're going to have to pay two dollars. That two dollars is going to be an annual thing because we're going to assume that's going to be our annual dividend of the two dollars. We're going to take the two dollars over forty. So to divide it by forty is going to give us our five percent.

So that's going to be our five percent. Now, this would be if there was nothing else involved here, this would be kind. Be our return, right, we would say, OK, you know, if we're going to pay two dollars annually and we're going to get the 40, then we're going to say to divide it by 40. And that'll give us our five percent that we can then use. But we also have the situation where and that would be kind of the cash. When you're thinking about the cash that's going out, we're thinking about the two dollars that are going to be paid. But there's also going to be that equity interest growth aspect of this due to them being the owners of the company. And we're seeing the growth that's going to be 12 percent. So we're also going to say the five percent plus that 12 percent expected growth in the five plus to 12.

That's going to give us our 17 percent. So you'll note here there's no tax implications because the dividends are something that are going to be paid, that are coming out of the equity balance sheet thing, not on the income statement as opposed to interest, which would be on the income statement. But we have this added factor, which can be a little bit confusing for us to calculate, which would be the expected growth rate in order to get a comparable rate, one that we can then kind of think about when we compare it to something like debt financing. Now, it's still not like a perfect comparison because, Of course, the expected growth is going to be something that's going to be highly speculative.

We've got to think about, you know, how much what's going to be the percentage ownership of the stocks that are going to be distributed as well. And we also note that the dividends could vary over time. Also, the dividends here are going to be something that could go on forever, considering the life of the company could in theory, go on forever. Whereas if we're looking at debt financing, we typically have some maturity date, even if there are 30 year bonds and whatnot, you would think there's some maturity date at some point in the future. So, Of course, our goal here is to come up with something that we can do a comparison with. And so this is going to be a useful tool for us to do those types of comparisons. So now we can say, well, what about the flotation costs? We'll do a slight adjustment to this to take into consideration now the flotation costs.

We got the same information. We're going to call it the cost of common stock. Now, as we add the flotation costs, the flotation cost is going to be the cost, like the one time cost of us to issue the stock and call it float. The stock was floating out there, apparently. So it's got the executive cause for us to get the stocks out there. So we'll take that one-time cost into consideration. It's different from the dividends in that the dividends are something we expect to be perpetual into the future. We're going to be paying dividends into the future, whereas the flotation cost is a one time cost, therefore will basically net it out against the price. So we're going to formula look something like this, dividends over the common stock price minus the flotation costs.

Then we're going to add the growth rate. So this little calculation will have a sub calculation in here taking care of that basically net sales price that will have. So what we have then is the dividends. We're going to have three columns now with the dividends in the middle column. So we've got the dividends and then we're going to compare that to the net price, not just the price at this time, which is going to be the net price, the common price, the common stock price to forty dollars like we saw before. But then taking out the cost of the issuance, the one time cost of the four dollars, the forty minus the four is the thirty six. So now we're going to be comparing the dividends per share to the net price, which is thirty six rather than the forty two divided by thirty six is going to give us five, five point five six percent.

Then we're back to basically the same area. We're going to take that five point five six. We're going to add then the growth rate which we're saying is the twelve percent and that'll get us up to then the seventeen point five six. So once again, a similar kind of formula. We just got to take into consideration the flotation cost. Note that that is a one time cost. Therefore, we're basically thinking that what we have received, even though we're selling for forty dollars, is basically the net sales price, which means we're going to be getting the thirty six in essence after that one time cost, then compare that to our dividends and then move forward in the same fashion as we did with the prior one.

Financing Common Stock Prob. 2

Up top information up here. We're going to calculate that information. Then down below, we're going to do the financing problem with relation to the common stock. Remember that you want to keep in the back of your mind financing options, common stock versus the debt type of financing debt that we've looked at in prior chapters that has a tax impact on it due to the fact that you typically will be paying interest, which is tax deductible generally when you're looking at the financing with common stock on the equity side, no tax consequence generally because it's coming out of the equity side of things. However, we do have the added complication when we're thinking about the common stock that is issued because we're basically having an equity interest or ownership into the organization.

Therefore, we have the cost that can be compared somewhat to the debt financing and that the payment that goes out could be the form of the dividend payment, but it comes out of equity and therefore it isn't having an impact on the taxes. And we also have to think about the growth in the value of the stock, considering the fact that there's an ownership interest. And if you think about the ownership interest in terms of just like the accounting equation, you have assets minus liabilities equals the equity interest. And that's what the stockholders basically represent to some degree. There are equity holdings. And we also need to consider the increase in that equity amount as to the value of what is being distributed so that we can then compare it possibly to other financing options, including possibly the debt financing.

So we have the dividends per year. We're going to say the four dollars. That's going to be the annual cost, that we're going to assume that the dividends are going out and we pay the four dollars on the dividend, the common stock price. This is what we're going to get per share that we issue. Also note that when we sell this common stock, this is a sale from the organization to finance the operations in the company, different from normal stock trades that happened on the stock market, which aren't all coming from the company, but typically are trades between individuals that that have already have the stock having been issued this, we're talking about the issuing from the company, the money from them still being paid on the market.

We're going to be getting this and sending it into the market here, trying to get the 90 dollars, selling them for as high as we can. But the money is going to go to the financing of the organization. The expected growth, we're going to say, is six percent. And then we have the flotation costs, which will be the costs of us to basically issue the stock. We'll talk about what will be before the flotation costs first, which we're going to call the cost of the retained earnings, which is going to equal the dividends. That's the annual cost divided by the common stock price, plus the growth rate. So that's going to be our calculation. We will do this a few different times. So we're going to go a bit faster to do so. We're going to put this into our table type of format here.

Dividends up top. It's going to be the four dollars that's going to be the annual kind of cost outflow that's going to happen in order for us to get the money for the issuance of the stock. Ninety dollars that we're going to receive per share and then the four dollars going out per share divided by ninety, it's going to give us the four point four four percent. So four divided by ninety four point four, four percent. That would be similar to what we would think of. It's kind of like a debt type of situation where we're saying, hey, this is what we're going to be paying in this case in dividends out of the company, leaving the company for the current cash per share of the ninety dollars. At this point, that means we have the four point four four percent divide in that out. But we also have an increase in the basic equity interest, which is six percent.

That's also the value that we're giving up here. So we want to add that as well. So we're going to say there's a six percent growth. We're going to add that as well. And once again, that's six percent difficult to come by. We'd have to do some estimates to see what that growth amount would be, but that's going to be our estimated growth. We're going to add that then to the dividends of the four point four four that gives us our ten point four four not perfect, but something that we can then compare a little bit more easily to something like the issuance of debt, other options we might have for the financing of the organization. It's not perfect because we're trying to get the best kind of tools that we can have. Also note the debt funding.

Scene will include a maturity date when you're talking about the interest, the interest usually not going on forever, even if you have 30 year bonds, it stops at some point in time, whereas the dividends do go on in theory, basically forever. The growth rate is something that we don't know for sure on the growth rate and and again, could go on forever. Basically, in theory, there could also be changes in the dividend. So note, we do our best to put the tools together so that we can basically compare apples to apples. Same thing, the same thing as best we can in this format. So they've got ten points four four. Then let's add on the flotation costs. So we'll just alter our formulas a little bit. We're going to call it.

The cost of common stock now equals the dividends divided by not just the common stock price, but the common stock price, minus the flotation costs, which is the one time cost of us to issue the stock, plus the growth rate. So we're then going to have the dividends per share for the same starting point. But now, instead of taking simply the price, we're going to get the net price, net price being the price, the ninety dollars minus the three dollars flotation costs, and that's a one time cost. So that means we're really only getting the eighty seven dollars after the cost of us just to simply issue the stock. Now comparing the four dollars divided by the eighty seven instead of the ninety, we're going to then be picking up the four point six and now we're in the same area we had last time simply adding on the expected growth.

The expected growth was the six percent to four point six plus these six percent giving us the ten point six. So slightly different than the ten point four four we had up top due to the flotation cost. Remember, the flotation cost is that one time cost. It's different from the dividends. That's acting as a cost. That's going to be the annual cost basically over time. So we're saying in order to get the eighty seven net sales price instead of getting the ninety, because that cost is happening at the point in time, we're basically getting the money and then comparing the four dollars to the eighty seven and then let's do it again. Just have a couple of examples. Let's say the dividends were one dollar and twenty cents. The common stock, meaning we're going to sell it on the market for fifty one dollars.

So in order to get fifty one dollars it's going to cost us one dollar and twenty cents. We're saying on the dividends expected growth was going to be a growth in the stock and thereby being a growth to the ownership of the stock for the common stock that is being issued for their percent ownership in the stock. We're going to say it's the eleven and then the flotation cost four dollars. We're looking first at the cost of retained earnings, not including the flotation cost here, that being the dividends divided by the common stock price that we sell, plus the growth rate. Putting that into the table, we're saying, all right, that dividends are going to be one point two. That's how much we're going to pay annually.

One dollar, twenty cents. And then we have the common stock price that we will compare it to issuing it onto the market for fifty one dollars. That's going to be the market price. Again, the money goes into the organization. So we're trying to get the money to finance the company. That's what we're trying to do here. So we got the one point two divided by the fifty one that's going to give us about two point three five percent. Then we're going to tack on and add on what we estimate the increase in the value of the company to be given the fact that the common stocks represent ownership in the company ownership and basically the equity ownership in assets minus liability, the value of the company. And we're going to say that that is going to be the eleven. So the eleven plus the two point thirty five is going to then give us the thirteen point thirty five note.

There could be some interplay, Of course, with the dividends and the expected growth of the stock. So, I mean, is the company holding on to the equity interest that they have to reinvest in the company, in which case the dividends you would think would be lower and the growth you would think would be higher? The expected growth would be higher, dividends lower? Or are they giving out larger dividends, possibly being a more established company, giving out the larger dividends and and and then possibly having a lower growth, basically stable type of situation in that situation? And then let's tack on the flotation, which changes the formula slightly, and we'll call that the account.

The cost of common stock equals the dividends divided by now, not just the price, but the price minus the flotation costs, basically the net sale price, plus the growth rate. So a similar process. We're going to see the dividends are going to be one point two against the same starting point. Now, we're going to calculate, though, the net price instead of just the price. That's going to be the common stock of the fifty one. And then we will have the four dollar floatation. Fifty one minus four is going to give us forty -seven. So in other words, instead of getting the fifty one dollars, we're basically getting the forty seven dollars now because that one-time cost of the four dollars for flotation to float out the stocks out of the market, I don't know why it's called flotation, but the.

US to issue the stock, so I'm imagining we float them out there might help you to memorize in order to float the stock out into the market so they don't sink. Then you have the flotation cost expenses. So then we got the one point two divided by the forty seven. That's going to give us the two point five, five percent. And now we're at the same point where we tack on or add on the expected growth, 11 percent to get up to the thirteen point five, five percent, slightly different from the thirteen point three four due to the one time flotation cost. Let's do it again, so now we got the dividends at the two point one common stock. It's going to be the twenty nine that we're going to issue for the expected growth, nine percent this time.

So dividends are a bit higher, expected growth a bit lower. We've got the flotation three dollars. So we will first calculate without the flotation, we're going to call that the cost of retained earnings, which would equal the dividends, divide it by just the common stock price instead of the net sales price plus the growth rate. So that's going to be the dividends per share, two point one in this case, that's what we're going to be paying annually, divided by the common stock price, how much we sell it for on the market. That's going to be twenty nine per share. So the two point one we're going to be paying each year divided by the twenty nine that we're going to get, it's going to give us the seven point two, four percent, then we're going to tack on or add on the nine percent expected growth, given the fact that this is an ownership percent and they're going to have a percent ownership in the company and therefore entitled to part of the growth is what we're giving up here.

So the seven point two four plus the nine percent gives us the sixteen point two four percent, which is a comparable percentage that we can at least use as a starting block point to compare against other types of financing options, including possibly debt financing. Let's take into consideration the flotation cost this time, shall we? We shall do that so we have the cost of common stock is what we're going to call it, dividends divided by basically the net sales price, this time not being the common stock price minus the flotation or one time cost of us to send these things and float them, float them out into the market. No one will buy them if they sink. So you have to make them float. So plus the growth rate, plugging that into our formula, we got the dividends per share is going to be the two point ten and then we're looking at net price this time. That's where we're looking.

That's where we're looking instead of just the price. So we got the common stock price at the twenty nine, but now we're taking into account the flotation cost so that we make sure that these things float out, they're gonna float. That's going to be three dollars. So that means the sales. So, you know, that's the cost of putting them out there. So we got the twenty nine minus the three is the twenty six. That's what we're basically going to get after the one time cost of the three dollars. Then we compare the two point ten to the twenty six that's going to give us the eight point eight percent. Then we're back to the same point, just simply tacking on or adding on the expected growth that this time or at the same time as the nine percent.

So the eight point eight percent plus the nine percent is now the seventeen point 08, slightly different to the sixteen point two forward due to the flotation cost of the three dollars. Let's do it again. OK, let's do it again. Get a little tired, but one more, at least one more. I've got one more in here. We're going to say the dividends this time, seven dollars common stock price. We're going to sell four of the fifty five dollars expected growth is seven this time. So expected growth is a little bit lower, the dividends a little bit higher. So maybe this is a more mature type of company, which basically they're not putting all the money back in because they're at the top of their kind of growth curve. But they're just running steady right now, given their money that they're making to the dividend holders flotation.

We're going to say six dollars to float these ones. Why are these stocks so heavy compared to them anyways? So first we're going to have it without the flotation. That's going to be the cost of retained earnings, which is going to be equal to the dividends divided by the common stock price, plus the growth rate. So that will be the dividends per share, seven dollar dividends. That's a big dividend. That's the annual amount that's going to be going out. And then we have the common stock price. That's how much we're going to get. Fifty five dollars that we're going to be selling these for. So the seven that's going to be going out yearly, we're assuming, divided by the fifty five. That's the twelve point seven three. Then we're going to tack on or add on the seven percent growth rate, given the fact that the people buying these stocks are going to have an equity interest.

And that's kind of like what the equity increase will be. That's part of what we're giving up. That's going to be seven dollars. So the twelve point seven, three plus the seven is going to give us in this case, nineteen point seven three nineteen point seven three. Let's add in this time the flotation cost, which we're going to call now the cost of the common stock. It's going to equal the dividends divided by not just the common stock price, but the common stock price, minus the flotation cost. And then we're going to tack on or add on the growth rate. So here we go. We got the dividends per share, seven dollars again, same starting point. But this time something new happened.

And that new thing is not just having the common stock price, but subtracting out the flotation cost, the six dollars to make sure these cost these things float out into the market and don't sink, meaning the costs for us to basically, you know, send out the stocks and whatnot, the executive costs or whatever, the admin cost. And that's going to be the forty nine. So if we take the seven divided by the forty nine, that's going to now give us the fourteen point two nine and then we add on or tack on it like that and tack on that. Some people might not understand anyway. Expected growth seven percent. So the seven percent plus the fourteen point two nine that gets twenty nine point twenty nine, that's close to the nineteen point seven three slightly different due to the rather high this time flotation costs. Let's do it again.

Weighted Average Cost of Capital (WACC)

When we have our financing options to finance the operations of the organization, we can break them out into basically two main categories. One being debt financing to equity financing. And when we make decisions on what we should be, fine, what our financing decisions should be, it can be useful for us to think about the weighted average between our methods to help us give us a baseline return that we would want to be receiving. So what we will do here, we can do this in different kinds of ways, this weighted average cost of capital. So we could spend a lot of time on the formatting of the formula. But we really want to just get an overall idea so that in future chapters we can get into many problems that will take a look at specific components, which will be things like the debt financing rate and the common equity financing rate.

So we can get into more detail on how to get to those components in future chapters, which can then be fit into a weighted average cost of capital kind of chapter or problem so that you can then think about what your financing options would be, and what would be the best financing options. So you could think about this in the format of a formula. So the formula would look something like this. E over D plus E times R E plus D plus E times R D times one minus T, where E is the market value of equity and the market value of debt and then R is the cost of equity and cost of debt and T is going to be the tax rate. This looks quite intimidating, but it's not too bad, although we could get into a lot of detail and we will in future chapters think about how we would get to each component of these items.

So you can kind of learn this conceptually and then drill into the details on how you would basically fill in each component. So when we look at different kinds of problems we will be focusing on different areas. Now, these weightings are E over D plus E. Note that debt and equity, if you think about the accounting equation, you've got assets, equal liabilities plus equity. So debt and equity you could think of as basically the value of the company. So if you're thinking about equity over D plus E, you've got your ratio analysis and the debt over D policy that's basically given here with our 40-60. So we're not going to be spending our time on really calculating these components. We're going to be basically spending our time thinking about the weights that we have here. So then the R.E.

Here, theRE is the cost of equity, which is given up top, and then the R d is going to be the cost of debt. When you do so these are going to be the two components that in future chapters will spend more time on drilling down and seeing. How would you get to these components? That's what future kinds of practice problems will be focusing on. So note that when you think about the debt financing, you could think about things like issuing bonds, for example. And when you think about the debt financing, you have an added problem. You might think, well, that's just going to be the interest rate, right? You might have the interest rate. You might have a problem between the market rate and the rate on the bond.

So usually we're going to use the market rate, but we'll see that in the future. But you also have a tax impact here because the interest will be deductible. So we've got to take that into consideration when we compare it to the equity financing, the equity financing being confusing in its own right, because that usually means we're giving an equity interest. The main thing we think about there is the common stock interest. So if we sell common stock, we have equity interest in the organization. And then the question is how do we value that? So we'll talk about how to value that in the future. We could basically present what we think of as the dividends that would be going out into the future and so on.

So we'd have to come up to the present value to get to what this percent would be so that we can then think about these two items and then plug it into our weighted. Average cost of capital type of formula to think about a baseline calculation that we want to get for a rate of return. So let's plug this into our formula here. I'm going to do this in a table type of format so you could basically plug it into a formula where you'd have the 60 40 for these items. And then you're looking at the R E and the R d, which would be the five and and 15 or 15 and five percent. Note here, however, this five percent, we're basically assuming that that has already been taken into consideration for the tax impact on it. So we're saying this is the debt financing rate after taxes, taking into account the tax consequences there.

So it looks something like this. We're going to say, let's pick up the wait. I'm going to say the weight of the debt, the weight of the debt is going to be 40 percent. I'm going to make that a percent by going into the home tab, go into the numbers group percent to find it. Then we want the cost of the debt. This is the percentage cost of the debt. It could be a little bit confusing to just be working with percentages, but we're trying to get that basically the rate of return that we want to have, which is going to be a higher return rate. So we'll practice using this kind of work within percentages. Then oftentimes when we can plug in actual numbers, like what are we talking about? How much are we borrowing here, then that can make it a little bit more concrete, which we will do in future chapters.

So the cost of debt we're going to say then, is that five percent. So we're going to take the no group and percentage by that. Let's go to the Ford group and underline let's call this a subtotal sub total. We'll bring this into the outside. This is going to be 40 percent times the five percent making that eight percent, no group percent to find it. It's going to be the two percent. I'm going to indent the subtotal alignment and indent there. We have our subtotal. So we basically took out our cost of debt times, the weight of the debt. And that's going to be the 40 percent that gives us the two percent. So now let's take a look at the weight of equity, weight of equity. This is going to then be equal to 60 percent. Note that these two, Of course, should be adding up to one hundred percent, the debt and the equity.

And so we're then going to make that a percent, no group and percentage by that. And then we're going to take the cost of equity. So say the cost of equity. Which we calculated to be the 15 percent per cent to find that number group per cent to fi and then for each group and underline will hit the subtotal, subtotal and dent that alignment and indent and then we'll multiply these out. So the 60 percent times, the 15 percent making that eight percent number of group percent to five Phonte groups and underline that's going to give us our weighted average cost of capital, which we're going to say is equal. Let's use this function. We're going to add these up equals to trustees, some function of the two and the nine, and that's going to be an 11 percent numbers group making that a percent at the 11 percent.

And that's kind of like our required rate of return. So if we're going to be investing in something and we're financing for that investment, we want to have a required rate of return, kind of like the floor of the 11 percent. If we're getting a return that's greater than that, then that's great. If we have a return that's less than that then we probably would be rejecting that project. And note, there's a difference in the financing options up here, because you're saying, well, if I have the debt financing, then it's only costing me the five percent here. And so if I have a rate of return of something over 11 percent, then I would still take on that job possibly. Right. We might put into that investment based on this calculation.

Other calculations would, Of course, be taken into consideration as well. But it's going to be if the return is above the floor, which is the weighted average cost of capital, the required rate of return, then we would basically pick up the job. Now, note, the thing that's a little bit funny here is even if you have the 15 percent item here and you had something that was greater than the required rate of return, meaning it's costing us in terms of equity, we're calculating at the 15 percent. But you have a return that's greater than the 12 percent, greater than 11. Then still, based on the weighted, it's still above the threshold.

Now, the idea here being that when we make our investment decisions, we would like to have a floor that we can have as something that we're going to be clear in in terms of the rate of return that we're going to have that will be somewhat independent from the type of financing that we're going to be putting into place. So that's going to be a that's going to make our investment decisions a bit more uniform in terms of our investment decisions. So that's one calculation that we can use basically among many. But then note, in future chapters, we're also going to be looking at this cost of debt. How do we get to that cost of debt and then the cost of equity? That's where our focus will be on future problems.

Now, note, it's also useful to see this in this kind of format. We can also put this in basically a table type of format, which would look something like this. We could say that we have the debt, say the debt and the cost of debt after tax. And remember, this number is basically the tax cost of debt. We'll talk more about what that means later. But there's a tax impact on the debt side, not on the equity side that we have to take into consideration. Home tab. No group is going from two percent to five. That weighted at the wait here for the debt, as we saw, was 40 percent. Let's make that a percent number group percent to find it. And then if we take the weighted cost the five times the 40 and make that a percent no group and percent to fight it, then we have the common equity financing, which I'm going to say is the 15 percent we said that was the 15 percent making that a percent, no group percent defined the weight that we have then for the equity we're saying is 60.

So making that a percent as well. Multiply that out 15 times the 60 making that eight percent, no group percent to find it. We've got that nine again. You could see the same kind of calculation. Some people like to see it in this table format. It's kind of a nice way to see it. So then we're going to go ahead and sum up the outdoor column equals to some of these two items and make that eight percent numbers group percent to find it. We can put an underline here under the nine if we want, and I kind of want it. So let's do a font group and then underline. So there we have that. Also note that these two should be adding up to one hundred percent. So Of course that's going to be adding up to one hundred percent. And there we have it. This could be a cleaner way for some people to see it.

Also note that you could add the preferred stock. We will talk about preferred stock in a weighting here as well if the preferred stock was applicable. But we won't get into that at this point in time. What you want to do is basically keep this weighting concept in mind when we go to the future problems as we focus on basically how do we figure out this cost of debt and how do we figure out the cost of equity numbers? Why would we want to figure them out? Because we're going to try to have to compare them when we think about different financing options. And then we might use them, Of course, for a calculation, for the weights to see, to try to balance out our ideal weights between our financing options as well.

Cost of Debt After Tax Prob 1

We have the debt financing we're considering here. We want to think about the cost of the financing and then the pros and cons, including the mix between debt and equity as we basically consider our financing types of decisions. So we also need to take into account when we're talking about debt financing, the tax impact of the debt financing, because taxes kind of turn everything on its head. They complicate things a lot in that for taxes, things that are bad or good, things that are good or bad and whatnot. So if we were to have debt, for example, we financed the debt and we might have to pay interest then on the debt that we have.

So we take debt and then we have to pay interest on the purchasing power of the debt that we have basically taken on that typically will take the form of interest, which is bad because that's like the rent that we're paying for the purchasing power that we have. But it's kind of good because it's an expense, which is basically a deduction for taxes. So we get kind of this tax benefit for this bad thing, kind of like the rent or interest that we're paying on the purchasing power of the money. So then the question is, well, what's the real impact or cost of the debt, given the fact that we have this tax consequence related to it? So here's are going to be our basic kind of example. The company can issue debt. They have the ability to issue debt, basically take on debt, increasing liabilities. The tax rate is. Thirty percent.

Also realized that when you talk when you're thinking about the tax rate, you could have a progressive tax system. So you might think, well, what would the actual tax rate be? It could be a little bit complex. When you're thinking about later decisions or decisions at this point, you're typically making them on the margin, as they say, in economics. So you're probably thinking about the last tax rate, the bracket that they are currently in, because that's when your current decision will be impacted means that meeting the highest tax bracket. However, if it's a big decision and you think it's going to be a more nuanced decision, they could have an impact on taxes of different brackets. For example, you could get more nuanced in terms of the tax calculation as well.

Just keep that in mind. So we're going to say that they could finance with five percent interest and the tax rate is going to be 30 percent. So we want to figure out the cost of debt after tax. So the after tax cost of debt, we can think of that from a percentage term without even thinking about the actual debt that we're trying to finance. And then I think most people would like to basically actually think through it with debt that they're going to finance. How much are they going to basically try to finance and have to pay the interest on? So first, let's think about it just in terms of rates, because that can be very useful in practice. So we could calculate the cost of debt after tax interest rate.

So let's pick up the interest rate, which is going to be the five percent over here, five percent going two percent to five, that by going into the home group or the home tab numbers group, percent to find it. Then I'm going to say that this is going to be one minus tax rate and that's going to be our subtotal calculation here. Colen to represent a subtotal calculation. So I'm going to say then one and then the tax rate is going to be 30 percent. So 30 percent on the tax rate. We're going to go to the numbers group and percentage IT font group and underline it. And then we'll take the one minus the tax rate. We're going to say this is equal to one minus the tax rate and go to the numbers percent to five. That and I'm going to call this a subtotal.

I'm going to indent these two alignments and let's go ahead and indent these so that we have that. So it looks nice. And then we have the cost of debt after tax. And I would call this like the percent basically, which is going to be then the five percent times the 70 percent making that, then a percent tab and adding then the decimals go into the numbers, adding a couple of decimals. Let's just add one decimal, the three point five percent going to put an underline here by going to the fourth group and underline. So if you think about this, analyze this quickly, then we'll do the example with actual things like imagining what the debt amount would be, come up to this number again, which I think will be more intuitively sound. And then you want to get back up here and basically understand this.

I'd better get it in your mind, because it is a useful calculation, so we got the interest rate that's going to be like the rent on the money. So we have to pay the interest for the debt. Then there's a tax impact because we basically get an expense, the expense going to be deductible for taxes. So if we're in a 30 percent tax bracket, then one minus the 30 is going to be the amount that's not going to be taxed. The 70 percent we take them to 70 percent times the five percent of the interest rate, then we have the aftertax percent affect the cost. Then instead of being five percent, the rent on money, instead of being five percent after the benefit of the taxes is really three point five percent, given the fact that we have the deduction.

Now, let's think about that by making an example here where we have a debt of one hundred thousand. I think that'll make it a little bit more concrete. So we're then going to say that the interest calculation interest, if we had this one hundred thousand to put interest Colan shift Colen and then this is going to be the debt pick up the debt here would say this equals the debt. I'll put this on the inside for a sub calculation of the one hundred thousand we're going to imagine that's how much we take out here. The rate is going to be the interest rate up top, going to pick that interest rate up at the five percent percent to five. The sell by go into the numbers group percent to five Fonte Group and then underline going to pull this into the outdoor column.

This is going to be one hundred thousand times the five percent. So that's the amount of interest. And that I think makes intuitive sense. Right. That's going to be the cost. I'm going to go to the home tab alignment, increase the indenting and then alignment, increase the indenting. That would then be the cost of the interest, the rent on the purchasing power of the debt that we have used in order to finance our operations. So then we're going to be picking up the tax benefit. So the tax benefit, let's say benefit shift, Kolan subtotal, this is going to be the interest. Let's call it the duck double interest expense now. So that's going to be the interest expense, which again, is good for taxes. So this is bad for normal. We have to pay five thousand. We don't like that.

It's like paying rent. Not good, but for taxes, good, because expense or deduction for us and then the tax rates. So what kind of tax benefit would we get? Won't tax that rate that we have multiplied times the tax rate over here. Let's pick that up on the side, which is going to be thirty percent. So we get a benefit of the five thousand times the 30 percent here numbers group, percent to five, we're going to bring this to the outside, the five thousand times the 30 percent, we get a benefit basically of the one thousand five hundred. So this is going to be the tax benefit. Let's call it a tax benefit, because that's what it is. That's why I call it that, because that's what it is. Alignment and dent. And then I'm going to indent this again.

So that's going to be the tax benefit. So the cost that we have in the cost of debt after taxes is really not just the five thousand that we're paying, not like the rent or interest, which is kind of like rent for the purchasing power of the three thousand five hundred, but minus the tax benefit. So really, given the fact that we reduced our taxes, the cost is going to be that three thousand five hundred. So that's kind of like a cost. But we might want to know that as a percent kind of calculation. Right. So now if I took them. Cost of debt after tax. Per cent, let's call it, we would then take the cost. Of the debt after taxes, which we just calculated, and compare it to the debt itself, the debt. Of the one hundred thousand, and that would then give us the cost of debt, After-Tax percent.

I'm going to call it, and let's indent these alignment and dent and dent this again. And then we're going to say this is going to be the three thousand five hundred divided by the one thousand. Add in a couple percent to find it. Adding a decimal and underline here might as well Fonte underline underline this one font and underline so that we get to the three point five. Now this is kind of a long process, but I think a lot of people, if they did it intuitively, they, they possibly do something more like this, imagining a debt that would actually be outstanding. It's quite useful, Of course, to then simplify the process with the process here where you don't even need to imagine a debt and just take the interest times one minus the the tax rate to get to the actual cost of the debt at the three point five, then then maybe you basically double check it with the example of actually putting in a debt. No.

To do that, to do the calculation. And that's useful to do when I mean, you want to mull it over in your mind a couple of different ways. So it's useful to put together examples that might make sense to you or make things quick in your mind. So let's do it over here. At example number two, we can imagine then the debt once again at the one hundred thousand one hundred thousand on the debt, if we imagine having a number for the debt, sometimes is useful to be able to figure these kind of calculations or make them make sense that your mind and then we're going to calculate the cost of debt after tax per cent and make this a percent. Colen, this is going to be a subcategory.

I'm going to take the interest rate, which I'll pick up over here, interest rate, and that's going to be the five percent. Five percent and let's go to the numbers group, make that then a percent and then I'll calculate this in one line here, the one minus the tax rate, one minus the tax rate. And that's going to be equal to one minus. The 30 percent make that a percent numbers group, percent defy Font's group and then underline and that'll give us the cost of debt after tax percent, but get rid of the colon in the end. I'm going to indent this alignment and dent and dent this one alignment and dent and then we can multiply this out. This is going to be the five times the 70 make this a percent numbers group per cent add a decimal three point five font group underline.

And then we're going to call this the cost of debt after taxes, which then will calculate at one hundred thousand times the three point five, and we get that three thousand five hundred that we got here. So sometimes reworking these examples down below can give us a better idea of the conceptual basically percent item that we have up top and make it a little bit more concrete in our mind, which I do recommend doing so that you could basically do something kind of like this. Right. The short calculation, if you actually had a debt that you need a number that you would need financed in your mind, you can run scenarios with a calculation that would probably be more like example number two here. And then you can basically do this short calculation, which is in essence the same thing up top.

So we'll do another example of this next time we do this just a couple more times. It is a crucial concept to understand. And when you're thinking about taxes, the question is when will taxes have an impact and then what? How you're going to calculate that impact. And when you're talking about financing taxes have an impact when you're talking about financing through debt, but not when you're talking about financing through equity. There's other costs related to equity. So we'll get to those later.

Cost of Debt After Tax Prob 2

We have the tax benefit related to that cost as well. So then we want to figure out, well, what's really the cost of the debt, if it's going to have a benefit for this tax benefit, the taxes often complicating the situation. Now, we can calculate this in basically theory on a percentage basis and then it's useful to think about the actual debt that you might want to finance and then think about it in that way as well. We'll work on a couple of different problems just if we can get this in our mind. So let's say that the company could basically finance debt at 12 percent so they could cost them 12 percent to finance it. The tax rate is going to be 26 percent. Remember that we do have a progressive tax rate.

So you might be thinking, is that the average tax? What is that? But normally, again, if you're making your decision on the margin, then you might be looking at the final tax rate, the end, the tax rate, rather than the average tax rate, because that's the tax rate that would be affected in your last decision. Possibly, but taxes can be a little bit more nuanced than that if you think it's going to have an impact on multiple brackets. So you gotta keep that in mind as well. We're going to take the twenty six percent here. So let's calculate basically the cost of debt after taxes will be basically the percent kind of calculation that we will get to which you would think the cost in the rent percent, 12 percent, but no tax benefit. Twenty six here.

So what then would be like the cost in terms of a percent? So we're going to say then we have the interest rate, let's pick up the interest rate column that's going to be equal to 12 percent. So let's pick that number then group or send to find that. Then we're going to take the subtotal, which is going to be one minus the tax rate. And I'm going to make a colon and make a little sub calculation, which will be one. And then we'll pick up the tax rate, which is going to be that. So 26 percent, 26 percent on the tax rate. So I'm going to make that eight percent go to the fourth group, underline it. So then we're taking one minus the tax rate. So we're taking one minus the tax rate. And we're going to go to the numbers group, make that eight percent.

And this is going to be a sub total, going to do some highlighting these sales alignment and dent making it look nice. Alignment and dent make an underlying here font and underline. Then we're going to be taking the 12 times the seventy for making that a percent numbers group percent define it and adding a couple of decimals were at the eight point eighty eight about again, a little difficult to understand this intuitively without basically having the debt calculation in there. You can memorize this formula and probably should, but you also kind of want to understand it intuitively here. So. Right. The interest rate is going to be the cost. That would be the cost. However, we get the tax benefit, we're taking one or one hundred percent minus the twenty six percent.

That leaves us the amount that we're not basically going to get back with regards to taxes. So when we pay the 12 percent, in other words, we're going to get a benefit of part of it. That's going to be the tax rate. At the twenty six, we're assuming one minus the twenty six gives us the amount that we're not basically going to get a benefit on the tax side from. So if we take the 12 percent of times that 74 percent, that's going to give us our rate of the eight point eight eight percent. So although the cost of debt, the interest we're going to have to actually pay 12 percent, the amount of the actual after tax costs, we're thinking is going to be the eight point eight eight. So we're going to call that the cost of debt after tax. And you might want to just put percent. I would call that kind of like the percent.

Now, it's useful to recalculate this with an example. So if you were to kind of move this over yourself, most people I think would come up with an example, give a debt example here, which would probably be more likely to happen in real life, or we're trying to finance a particular amount and then and then figure it out, something like this, where it's the area where the interest I know if I had debt that I was taken out would be the one hundred thousand that I'd have to be that. That's how much money I want. And the. Most of that typically would be the rent, the interest on it, and I know that's what I'm going to have to pay. So I'm going to assume it's 12 percent that we have to pay. That's the rent on the purchasing power.

So normally, if taxes weren't messing everything up, it would just simply be the interest would then be the one hundred thousand times twelve and that would not be a problem. But then we have the taxes that messed everything up. So let's go to the alignment and dent this and indent this so that I'm going to say now what's the tax benefit? So the tax benefit benefit would then look something like this. We'd have the interest, which now would be the interest, expense or deduction. So I might even call it that. Let's call it interest expense deduction. Now that we have is going to be that 12000 that we get from taxes. That's good for taxes. It's bad. But like for taxes, it's good because taxes or taxes are weird. So the tax rate, we're going to get a benefit of twenty six percent on the tax rate because it's deductible.

And so we're going to go to the numbers group percent to five, that font group, underline, underline, and then that's going to be the tax benefit. So we'll say tax benefits and multiply that out. So that's going to be twelve thousand times to twenty six percent. So let's do some indentations here, go into the alignment and dent that one and then into that one. So then let's underline this one, go into the font group and underline so underline that and then. We're going to say that we have the cost of debt after taxes would then be the rent of the twelve thousand minus that three one two zero. So the real cost to us in terms of dollars with this example would be eight thousand eight eighty.

Now, if I want to think about that in a percent type of format, we can then say, OK, well, what's the cost of debt after tax percent than coal? And we then go, all right. Well, that's going to start off with the tax benefit. Let's just take the tax benefit of that eight zero and compare that to divide the 1000 cost of the debt. And then that's going to give us our cost of debt, After-Tax percent like so, percent like so and we'll indent this alignment and dent and then and dent this one again. This should be a capital C, and then we're going to say this is going to be the eight eight eight zero divided by the one hundred thousand percent to find that numbers group percent to five underline groups and underline add in a couple of decimals here.

So we'll just normalize this, add in a couple of decimals, let's give it a double, underline two. So there we got the eight point eight eight on that one. And then I think it would be useful to when you actually do this in practice, if you have the debt amount, you might do a calculation like this. You'd be saying, well, here's the debt. One hundred thousand on the debt again. And then my calculation, if I pull out the cost of debt, After-Tax percent coal, and that would be the interest rate, the interest rate is going to be equal to 12 percent. And that I would like to be able to go right to. No, Stroope percent defy the calculation of one minus the rate, the tax rate, tax rate.

And then that's going to be equal to we're going to say one. Minus the tax rate, which is 26 percent. That will then give us a five percent to five that PHONTE group underlying this that's going to give us our cost of debt after tax per cent. Pulling that out to the outside, the 12 times the seven for making that into eight percent, adding a decimal or two, and this calculation right here basically mirrors what we did up top here. And that would give us then our end result, no less indent this alignment and dent here and dent this one, make this see a large C otherwise known as the capital. And this is going to be the cost of debt after taxes, which would then be one hundred thousand times the eight percent in terms of a dollar amount.

Let's go ahead and underline this. Let's do the double underline here. The W. Double the underlying OK, so there we have that, let's do it a couple more times here, because that was good. That was fun. And so I want to do it again. So down here, same kind of concept, different different numbers so the company can issue debt interest rate, 10 percent. Now we're going to assume the tax rate. We're probably thinking about the last tax rate, the marginal tax rate, making the decision on the margin at thirty two. So let's think about the cost of debt after tax percent. We're going to say let's do this again, interest rate. And it's how you get good at this. You just do that when you do this like a million times until you're good at it.

And then we got the 10 percent percent to find that number group percent to five subtotal, which is going to be the one minus the tax rate and shift zero colon. And then this is going to be one tax rate is going to be equal to thirty two percent this time going to go to the numbers group percent to five and then Phonte and under line there's a line underneath and this is going to be a subtotal. Pulling this into the outside. We've got one. One hundred percent minus the thirty two percent, and making that a percent to five numbers, that leaves us with the sixty eight percent. So we've got 100 percent minus the thirty two, which means we have sixty eight amounts, basically that it's not going to be we're not going to get back on basically a tax deduction kind of concept. Right. So we had 100 percent minus the tax rate. Sixty eight.

And we're going to underline that font group and underline so that if we take the cost which would have been the 10 percent and multiply it times, the one minus the tax rate, we're thinking the cost is actually the seven point or six point eight zero percent. And this is the cost of debt after tax percent. And let's give a double underline. Here, so, like so. OK, and then we could go. We can do this calculation, same type of thing, go with our example down here. If I was to do this intuitively, I would probably start with a debt amount. In practice, we would probably know how much we want to borrow or I might just use that and say, OK, well, if I had the interest on the debt I'm going to try to get it is like one hundred thousand. And the rate of interest if I'm not taking the taxes into account is simply going to be the interest rate of the 10 percent. And that's straightforward.

If it wasn't for taxes messing everything up. So that would be no. Stroope underlying Phonte group underlined the first one as a percent, not an underlying. This would be the interest. And multiply that out in the water column. So that would mean that this would cost me 10 percent if it wasn't for taxes so alignment and didn't go in here alignment. And then I would probably think like, all right, well, what's the tax benefit then? Tax benefit. Let's do that, that would be like the tax deduction, which would be interest expense deduction. So this is like ten thousand rent on the money, the interest on the money. What we have to pay is bad. But for taxes, it's good because taxes are weird, taxes are weird.

And then why is tax weird? That's going to be the 32 percent benefit making that van a numbers percent define it. And this is going to be the tax benefit and that's going to be equal to the ten thousand times the 30 to underline here for that group and underline and let's go ahead and indent these guys alignment and indent and then indent again alignment and then indent. Then we have the we can think about this in terms of the cost of debt after taxes, in terms of dollar amount is the ten thousand minus the tax benefit, which really only costs us six thousand eight hundred. After we do the taxes, then we can go, OK, well what's the percent benefit then.

So I could say, OK, well what's the cost of debt after tax percent then? And that then is going to be the cost of debt after taxes is going to be that six eight. We're going to compare that to the debt dividing. When I say compare divides, that's what we're doing. One hundred thousand. And this is going to give us the cost of debt after taxes, tax percent, putting that in the outer column, that's going to be the six eight divided by the one hundred thousand percent to find eight percent if I add a decimal or two. So there we go. Let's make this an indentation, go into the alignment indent and line and indent this one again.

Now, you want to do a quick calculation, most likely in practice, it might look something like this instead of doing this whole thing, which I probably would do this whole thing just to double check it. But you could get there a little quicker. You're saying, OK, well, if the debt that I'm taking out is one hundred thousand. And then I'm just going to go right to right to this end result of the six five, what's going to be the cost in terms of a dollar amount? What's going to be the cost of debt after tax percent? Then let's get right to there, which is basically this calculation we did up top, a little bit simplified or a little bit condensed. Let's say. We'll say the interest rate is going to be the 10 percent that would be the cost if there were no taxes. But there are taxes.

Taxes are a thing in the world. Death and taxes. They are things that are real and we have to deal with them. So one minus the tax rate, and that's going to be equal to one minus the tax rate. And then we're going to go to the numbers group and percent defy that and then let's underline it and underline it, and that's going to be the cost of debt after tax percent pulling out to the outer Collum. We're taking the 10 percent times the amount basically after that, not included in the tax rate, one hundred percent minus the tax rate or the sixty eight percent in this case. And that's going to give us then if we go to the numbers group percent to fight at a couple of decimals, we're back to that six point eight zero font group underline.

Then we can multiply this out and say, well if it's one hundred thousand, the real cost isn't 10 percent, but that six point eight, which means it's going to cost us six thousand eight hundred. And let's go ahead and dent these here alignment and dent and then indent again. And this is going to be then I'm going to call this the cost of debt after taxes. Now, this is a pretty calculation that's going to be an easier one to do. Notice this one gives you a lot more information, actually. So in practice, if I'm really analyzing something, I might do the full thing here so I can basically say, OK, that's the rent. You know, that's how much after the rent, the benefit after and then the percentage amount this is actually could give you useful more information.

But when you're doing a comparison between two kinds of competing types of financing, you might just want basically the cost in terms of a percent. And if you're given an example, you want a quicker calculation, you should be able to get to it in this format as well, which, Of course, would also be easier to do if you're doing like a test question, your time is a constraint. OK, let's do this one more time. This is the last time that we have to do this and we're going have to stop. So you want to make sure you're picking up the full enjoyment of it this time because it's the last one. So we got the interest rate going to be eight percent this time. Tax rate now is at 40 percent. So let's calculate it with our cost of debt after tax with let's just do the percent. We don't even need the actual debt in this one.

So we're going to say this is going to be the interest again, interest. I'm going to put this outside. That would be the cost if there was no tax effect. That's like the rent on the purchasing power of the money that we're using to finance the organization. But then we're going to take that time. The one minus the tax rate, one minus the tax rate. I'm going to put that in a subtotal indicating that with a Colon and then we're going to save one and then the tax rate, which is going to be equal to 40 percent. So one is obviously one hundred percent minus the 40 percent here. You can make that a percent this time, if that would be useful. Let's make that a percent. Let's underline here Phonte Group underline and then this is going to be then I would just call it the subtotal because it's the total underneath subtotal. So this is going to be the one hundred percent minus the 40 percent.

So again, you can think about this a couple of different ways just to make it make sense in your mind. You might think of it like one hundred percent of the debt, for example, minus the 40 percent of the debt, which means that the 40 percent representing in this case, what you're kind of actually going to get back in terms of taxes, you're going to have to pay the full one hundred percent. You're going to kind of get 40 percent back with regards to a tax benefit. If we make the numbers and percent to five, that means we're left with a 60 percent, the 60 percent debt, which we're not going to basically kind of get paid back in terms of a tax benefit. So if we take that 60 percent times the rate, then the cost that we have in total, 60 percent times the rate is going to be then the numbers group percent to find five percent add in a couple of decimals. We're looking at four point eighty four point eight.

Let's underline here, go into the font group and underline so that we have that let's do some alignment aligning out this one and put the subtotal out there. And then we're just going to call this the cost of debt after tax. And I'm going to say percent here, percent. So like so OK, then let's do our examples down below. This would be the long example, which I think would be the most intuitive and might give you more information in practice where we would actually assign a debt amount. And in practice you might actually have a debt amount where you could basically do the calculation with a debt number, which can be more intuitive and give you a little bit more detail about what might be going on. So let's calculate the interest then. If I know what the debt is, then I'm going to say if it's debt, it's going to be one hundred thousand.

And I'm going to say, well, that's not the hold on a second. We're going to say the debt is going to be equal to 100,000 and then the interest rate is going to pick up. If I can finance it for the eight percent, then I'm just going to pick up that eight percent less percent to five. That number is group percent to five fought group underline. And then this will be called the. To rest, putting that on the outside, the one hundred thousand times, the eight percent that would give us the eight thousand of the cost, then I'm going to go ahead and indent here, go into the alignment and dent interest and indent that again. Then we could think, OK, what's the tax benefit tax benefit on this?

And I could say, well, that's going to be the interest expense, interest expense or deduction, which is going to be that eight thousand, which is now good because it's for taxes now.

So bad things are good, good things are bad taxes. And we're going to say tax is 40 percent. 40 percent. And so now we're going to say numbers underline Phonte I'm sorry, percent and then underline and then we're going to say this is going to be the tax benefit in effect, and that'll be equal to eight thousand times the 40 percent. So three thousand two hundred on the tax benefit. Let's go ahead and indent here. Alignment and dent and then and dent this one again. And then I'm going to say, all right, well, then what's going to be that's going to give us the cost of debt after taxes on a dollar amount basis, which would simply be the eight thousand minus the three thousand two.

So it's not going to cost us a thousand as it would if it wasn't for taxes. We're thinking we're going to get three thousand two of it back in the form of basically taxes or tax deductions or reductions. And then we're going to say then, well, what's the cost as a percent cost of debt after tax percent? This is useful because it's useful to compare to other kinds of things as a percentage oftentimes. So I'm going to say, all right, well, then we're going to say, let's pick up the cost of debt after taxes, which is the four thousand eight, and compare that to the debt meaning divide. That's what COMPAR was going to mean typically. And that's going to give us then the cost of debt after tax per cent. I'm going to call it. And let's go ahead and indent here.

We're going to go to the alignment and Dent and Dent again. This is going to be then the four thousand eight hundred divided by the one hundred thousand making that eight percent number group percentage by adding some decimals too. And then I'll underline it here. Font group underline I'm going to double underline their double D underline. There we have it again. Let's do it this way. Now, this is probably the shorthand way. If you actually have the debt, which will kind of implement this calculation in it, we'd say, all right, if we had the debt then and we knew that was like one hundred thousand, I could shorten up this calculation by basically just getting right to the cost of debt after tax per cent here, which it would be the interest rate. That interest rate times are tough, times one.

I'll make it one minus the tax rate, tax rate, and so we got the interest rate, which is going to be then equal to the eight percent annual percentage. By that numbers group and percentage by then, this is going to be equal to one minus the tax rate. And we're then going to go to the numbers group percent to five. We're basically doing this calculation up top now, Phonte group and then underline, underline in here. And that's going to give us the cost of a jet. After tax per cent per cent, and then we have that pulling out to the outside, the eight percent times, the 60 per cent per cent a fine that goes into the numbers grew per cent to five and then adding some decimals.

So we're at eight point four. And then let's end this one, go into the alignment and dent and then intent. And now that this calculation right here is basically a shorthand of this. And if we actually have the debt, then we can calculate that against the debt, which would be the one hundred thousand times that four point eight getting us to that four thousand that matches this number that we did and that this format. And this is going to be what we'll call the cost of debt after taxes. And let's go ahead and underline here Ford Group underline. And there we have it.

Cost of Debt After Tax Interest Rate Calculation

We have a similar type of situation with many kinds of areas within finance that we don't really want to memorize another formula. We just want to note that this falls into a particular formula. Look for that unknown user algebra in order to solve for that unknown. So what we have here, the cost of debt after taxes. So this is not the interest rate, but the cost of debt after taxes. So the interest rates are going to be something higher than that. We know the tax rate is thirty five percent and then we'll have our example problem down here where we'll have the date, the debt of one hundred thousand. But let's first just consider these two pieces of information.

So we're going to plug this into our formula, looking for the interest rate. We're not looking to basically memorize another formula. We want to just note that this plugs into our normal formula here, which is the cost of debt after tax calculation, which would be the debt rate or the interest rate times one minus the tax rate. In this case, the cost of debt after taxes is known, which would be the 10 percent equals the debt rate, the unknown right here, times one minus the tax rate, 35 percent known. Once we put that into our algebraic equation, we can solve for the debt rate the unknown and work the algebra to figure it out. That way, I'm going to use our tables to kind of figure this out up top.

And once again, I'm going to format the table as I normally would, and not rework the equation algebraically to solve for the debt rate. And then think about how we can kind of back into the debt rate in this format. So we could say the interest rate, normal calculation would be the interest rate, interest rate, and that's the unknown. So I'm going to put that on the outside. That's what we do not know. I'm going to just make up an interest rate right now just to complete the calculation point one. And then we're going to have the calculation of one minus the tax rate. Let's do it this way, one minus the tax rate. Colin. And hold on a second. There we go, so we're going to say one and then the tax rate is going to be equal to thirty five percent. I'm going to make both of these percentages by now.

So we got one hundred minus the thirty five underlining this. And let's not underline this one, only underlining the second one. And that's going to give us a subtotal, which I'm going to put outside. This is going to be the one hundred percent minus the thirty five percent making that then eight percent, no group percent find it. I'm going to indent these two alignment and dent subtotal and dent again here. And so then I'm going to underline the sixty five underline here and this is going to give us our cost of debt after tax so we know what this answer is. This should be the 10 percent. So if we know what that is, I'm going to make this a percent. No group in percent. We can kind of back into the answer up top rate because this time this should give us the 10 percent.

So we should be able then to take this equals than this divided by this should give us some. So one more time. This should equal that divided by this should give us our fifteen point thirty eight so we can see, even if you see a kind of basic calculation like this, to just formatted in the normal table kind of format and back into it, you can also use the goal. So the goal seeking any kind of situation like this, we'd say, OK, it's zero point one. This wouldn't be as useful in a test scenario, but it could be useful in practice when you have a worksheet or something that you're working with commonly and you would say, OK, normally it would be this 10 percent. I just made up 10 percent of the sixty five.

And then I want this number to be ten here so I can use Google, seek to change this cell to get to the end number, to what we need it to be by going into the data data tab, the what if analysis goal seek. We want to set this cell to be the point one point one by changing then the 10 percent up top, and then we're going to say, OK, so then that's another way we can basically find this item up. Now let's do the algebra, rework the algebra here, solve for the debt rate, and then I'll just take another table down here, which will basically give us the bottom line number of being the debt rate. So let's solve this. We're going to say then the cost of debt after tax then is going to be the 10 percent. This is going to be the 10 percent that we know. We're going to make that then eight percent by going to the home tab numbers, percent to find it.

And then we have the same information here, which is going to be the one minus the tax rate, which is going to be the one end in the tax rate. Same thing here. And that's going to be equal to the 35 percent, 35 percent less percentage by these two by go into the numbers group percentage by going to underline the second point font group and underline and that'll give us then our subtotal call it subtotal, which is going to be the one hundred minus the thirty five and making that a percent numbers group percentage find it going to grab these two and then alignment and dent on the line. The subtitle again and indent it again. That'll give us the end result then being the debt rate, the debt rate which will be equal to the 10 percent divided by the 65. And then I'm going to make that a percent.

No group percent defines it and adds some decimals. There will add a few decimals. So there we have it once again. Let's put an underlying thought group and underline. So this would be the most straightforward way to do it. All we did was rework basically the algebra of this equation, plugging in for the unknown, solving for the unknown, reworking our table for the debt rate. Now, let's just plug this back into our longer example and imagine we know what the debt is: this one hundred thousand, because sometimes this makes it a little bit more concrete when you're not just talking about percentages and you basically add the debt in there.

So if I didn't, like, understand or remember these two formulas, I might then say, well, what if the debt let's apply an amount to the debt and kind of think through it so we would have our kind of our longer type of format here and make this a little bit smaller so we can see this. This is going to be the interest calculation and I'm going to say the debt. Then let's pick up the debt. Which we're going to imagine this time to be the one hundred thousand multiplied that times, the rate, the interest rate, let's say interest rate, which is what we don't know. So I'm going to make up a number here. I'm just going to make up the 10 percent, again, 10 percent I'm going to put there for now.

That would give us the interest then the interest that we'll calculate, which will be one hundred thousand times that 10 percent. So that's the normal calculation that we would normally kind of go through. I'm going to then select these items, go to the alignment and don't be interested down here and indent that again. Then let's calculate the tax benefit based on what we know, tax benefit benefit. And that would be then the deep, dark, double interest, which now would be that ten thousand times the tax rate is what the benefit would be. So that tax rate would be thirty five percent making that eight percent number three percent to find it.

group and underlining that's going to give us our tax benefit on the outer call the 10th that this should be ten thousand times the thirty five percent, that deductible interest times the tax rate and that would be the in this case the three thousand five hundred underline font group and underline. Let's indent these three by going into the alignment and dent tax benefit alignment and dent again. So that's going to give us then our cost of debt after taxes, which is going to be then the ten thousand minus the three five, assuming the 10 percent as the interest rate. So then if we wanted to calculate our percent cost of debt after taxes in a percent format, the cost of debt after tax per cent then.

Is going to be let's make this a percent per cent colon is going to be the cost of debt after taxes, which is going to be that 65 compared to the debt itself, compared to the debt itself, which is the one hundred thousand. And then we'll subtract those that will divide those out. This is the cost of debt, after tax percent. And then I'm going to get rid of the colon on the end here. And let's indent these go into the alignment and dent and dentin again, alignment and dent again. We're going to then take these six five divided by the one hundred thousand percent to find that number is three percent to five. It adds a couple of decimals, underlining the one hundred thousand font group underline. OK, so then we can basically kind of back in then and say OK, that 10 percent, what does it need to be to get to the bottom line number, this one where we need it to be, which is that 10 percent.

So this 10 percent is just a random number and we're trying to get the bottom line to be that 10 percent. So I could then change this to 11, but not that one. Hold on. Undo, undo. I could then change this one up here to like 11 percent and so on, 12 percent until the end number gets to where we need it to be. I can basically make an algebraic equation out of this if I wanted to, and then basically solve for the unknown up top. Or we can use Google Seke if we had an Excel worksheet in order to figure this out once again, that would not be as appropriate to do. You can't do that in a test situation where you don't have Excel and Gozi, but it could be useful to work in different ways in Excel.

So you have a better understanding of it in your mind what it actually means, which helps to commit it to memory and then and then be able to rework these problems easier, having a better understanding of them. So in any case, I'll do the Google sneak up top. We're going to go seek what if goal seek and we'll just say let's change this cell to b point one by then adjusting this cell and say like, OK, let's do it. And there it is. It's been done. We wanted to do it and now it's done. So there it is on the 10 percent.

Calculate Bond After Tax Cost to Issue

There's going to be a tax consequence on it as well, because the cost of the bond, the interest that we have to pay on the bond will typically be deductible, which is actually good for taxes. Therefore, their cost is not simply on a percentage basis the percent of interest, but it's going to have to be adjusted for the tax benefit that will be involved as well. Bonds are also a little bit more complicated in that we have two rates that we're talking about. We're talking about the rate of interest that will be paid on the bond. And we also then half the rate is that is the market rate that we have to consider those two things, possibly not being the same. If they're not the same, then the bond will generally have been issued at either a premium or a discount in order to issue the bond.

So then the question is, Will, what do we use when we're trying to figure out the cost on a percentage basis? And the answer is typically going to be the market rate. And that might sound a little bit unusual because you're saying, hey, look, the interest that we're actually paying, it's going to be based on basically the rate on the bond. And in this case, we don't have the rate. They just have the payments, which we're saying are ninety dollars. That's different from the market rate. But basically what happens if you think about it from an accounting type of standpoint, when you issue the bond at a premium or a discount, you then have to amortize the premium or discount and typically that will result in the other side going to interest expense.

So ultimately, you kind of are using the market rate if you sell it as a premium or a discount. And so that's why that would be a good estimate in order to use rather than the rates on the bond, even though the actual payments you're making once you get going are going to be at the rate on the bond. The difference between the premium and the discount and the rate and the face amount of the bond is basically due to interest. So let's see that a little bit more clearly here. We have our information on the bond outstanding, we're saying it had a par value of one thousand the year to maturity. It's going to be twenty five annual interest payments, we're going to say 90. So we don't have the rate given here.

We just said the payment is going to be 90 and then the current market price, we're saying is nine hundred and thirty. So you could see this being issued then at a discount down below will work, basically the same situation, but this wouldn't be an issue basically at a premium. So this one's going to be issued at a discount. We know the tax rate is going to be thirty five percent. So now we want to figure out basically what's the percent cost after taxes. This one's been a little bit more complex in that we don't know the market rate. We've got to figure out the market rate first. If they had given us the market rate, then we could do a calculation similar to that we had seen in the past. If we're not given the market rate in this case, we're given the price and we have to back into the market rate.

We've got to first do something we've seen with the bonds in our bond chapter. So we've done more problems on this, on basically when we thought about bonds to figure out what the market rate would be based on the price, then we're going to take that market rate as opposed to the rate on the bond to help us to then figure out what the cost of the of the debt after tax would be. So if we're trying to figure out the market rate, there's a couple of ways we can do it. I think the more intuitive way would be to figure out the price here normally would be to take the annuity and then add the present value of one, the annuity of present value in the annuity payments, the interest payments present value in the payment of one at the end of the bond.

Add in those two up and then use basically Goolsbee to figure out what the actual rate is. Or we can use the rate function even if you use the rate function. However, I would still double check it basically with this first method here. So let's first use the goal seek method. I think this is the most intuitive method. It's difficult to do this mathematically because basically we have two things going on, an annuity and a present value of one calculation. So algebraically it gets a little bit complex, obviously, with Excel. And so it's a lot easier to kind of work out. So in this case, let's just imagine that the rate is going to be, let's say, five percent of five, and then use that to calculate the total down here, which would be the price.

And then we'll adjust this using Google, seek to figure the price at the nine thirty, then we'll do the same thing with the rate from. So let's use the present value calculation equals the present value shift nine, we're going to take the rate which we're estimated to be that five percent comma number of periods.

We're going to say twenty five. We're assuming it's an annual interest bond, comma. And then the payments that we're going to have are going to be ninety dollars. Ninety dollars because they gave us the payment, not the interest rate. If they give us the rate, we'd have to take the rate on the bond times to one thousand. That's going to give us a positive number by going back into it.

I'm going to put a negative side before the P to make it a positive number. Let's do the present value of one present value in this one thousand with our assumed rate of the five percent negative present value shift nine rate is going to be that assumed five percent comma number of periods is going to be twenty five comma comma future value. We're going to be picking up that one thousand and entering. So if we add those two up we get a price based on that five percent rate of the one five six three seventy six. Now we need it to be nine hundred and thirty. I can then change this percent here to get closer and closer to what it should be. Right.

We got eight and so on and so forth. I can use Google seek to then do that for me, go into the data tab, go into the what if analysis goal, see, and we want to set then this cell to be what we know. It should be that nine thirty, which I have to hard code here, nine three zero by then changing the rate over here. And then we're going to say, OK, do that list and there it is. So the rate would be that nine point seven six. Now we can do that a little bit more easily with the rate function and excel. I'll just type in the rate function this time. We have to be careful with negative numbers as we use the rate to function, however. So I'm going to say this is going to be equal to the rate shift nine and the number of periods I'm going to pick up the twenty five comma. The payment that we're looking for is going to be the 90 and I think that needs to be a negative 90.

That's where the trickiness comes in. Comma, if you don't put the proper negatives in, it will give you the proper answer. And then the present value we're saying is the 930 comma future value. I need a negative here, I believe as well of the one thousand there, and that should do it for us. Enter a notice that gets there a lot faster than doing this calculation. However, I would still double check this calculation by doing the this this present value of the annuity using that rate and the present value of one just to double check that you do indeed get to that 930 again once we have this amount, the nine seventy six, which is the market rate, because the market rate is what's going to determine what we have to issue the bond for in this case at a discount, and that the difference between that discount is going to be basically work itself out with interest payments as we then amortize the discount over the life of the bond.

So we're not using the bond rate, which in this would be ninety divided by one thousand or nine percent. We are instead using the nine point seventy six percent market rate, even though when we pay the interest payments, we're paying the ninety dollars due to the fact that the difference is really basically interest that we will record. And in the format of interest, basically when we amortize the discount that we had to put in place, when we basically sold the bonds for nine hundred thirty and then have to pay at the end of the time period, one thousand at the end. OK, so now, so now we can just do our normal type of calculation. Now that we have the cost, this would normally be what we consider the cost to be if there were no taxes. Now we have to include taxes.

So we're going to separate. So the interest rate and I'm going to say market rate is going to be then this nine point seventy six, making that a percent percent to find it, add a couple of decimals, then we're going to take the one minus minus. That's not a minus tax rate shift of nine Kolan. That's going to be one. And then the tax rate. So I'm going to say the tax rate is going to be then thirty five percent here. Thirty five percent. I'm going to buy these two sales. No group percentage by them. Underline here font and then underline, subtract those out. This is going to be one hundred minus thirty five. Let's put that in the outdoor column, the one hundred minus the thirty five making that eight percent number of group percent defined it and this is going to be a subtotal and then that's in these two over here alignment and dent and dent this one alignment indent.

And then down here we're going to call this the cost of debt after tax which is going to be equal to the nine. Point seven, six times the sixty five, and we're going to go to the numbers group percent to defy that, add a couple of decimals. We're looking at six points three four. So this would be the market rate. This would be what we think the cost is after we take into consideration the tax impact. The nine percent nine divided by the one thousand would be the actual rate on the face of the bond. So it gets a little confusing. Their home tab fight group underlines if we try to plug this into our longer basic example and think about what the actual calculation would be. It looks something like this.

As we've seen in prior chapters, we can calculate the interest, which is basically market using the market rate shift. And then this is where the confusion kind of lies here, because the interest you're saying would be the one thousand I'm sorry, the one thousand let's just call it the death of one thousand is going to be the face of the bond that would be owed at maturity. And then the interest rate would be market rate. And again, you would think, why is it at ninety nine, nine ninety divided by one thousand, the rate on the bond. Why isn't it nine? Because even though we're paying ninety dollars, which is nine thousand times the rate on the bond, the difference between the two is going to be amortized out.

So the real rate that we're paying because we sold it at a discount is the market rate and that's the confusing component here. So we're going to say market rate. Then it's what we have to use there that would give us the interest. So we got the one thousand times the market rate and then I'm going to add a couple of decimals numbers, add in a couple of decimals. Also note that when you're using that market rate, then it's a little confusing to tie it out to each period that is going to be covered, depending on how you amortize the discount or premium. Anyway, let's leave it at that. We're going to then highlight these three. We're going to go to the home tab alignment indent, then we're going to go to the alignment and indent here again, the tax benefit tax benefit.

And this is going to be the interest expense. Let's call it expense deduction so we can deduct the interest expense. That's going to be like the benefit here, which is going to be that ninety seven, fifty seven basically on average over the life of the fund.

We're going to then say numbers first, let's make that a couple of decimals and then we're going to say the tax rate tax rate is going to be this 35 percent percent to find that number is group percent to five. Underline font group underline. We're going to take then the ninety five, fifty seven times that thirty five percent add a couple of decimals, no group decimals in it. And then we're going to say that that is the tax benefit. And let's do some indentations here, selecting these three alignment and dent tax benefit alignment and dent.

So that's going to be that. And then we're going to have the cost of debt after taxes on a dollar basis is going to be on average the ninety seven fifty seven minus the thirty four fifteen. Add in some decimals, no group couple decimals underline in this one font group underline and then we can take a look at the cost of debt after tax people cold and calculate the cost of debt after taxes being that sixty three forty two. Comparing it to the debt faced amount here that we have to pay at maturity. The one thousand add in a couple of decimals to the sixty three numbers group couple decimals underlining font group and underline. And then this is going to be the cost of debt after tax per share and this is going to be equal to the sixty three forty two divided by the one thousand making that a percent, no group percent define it.

Add in a couple of decimals. We get once again to that six point three four six point thirty four. Let's indent here alignment and dent and dent this one alignment and dent. OK, let's do this again. We'll do it a bit quicker here. This time we have a discount situation here. Let's do the same thing where we have basically a premium type of situation. So note that the rate on the bond was nine percent still just as it was here. Ninety divided by the one thousand nine percent last time we came up to a market rate that was higher, resulting in it having to have been issued than at a discount. So at this time, we're expecting it to be issued basically at a premium. It has been issued at a premium. So we expect the rate, the market rate then.

To be lower than nine percent, so let's do that calculation, let's do that goal kind of component first, I'm just going to like, yes, a number over here to start off, just like we did last time. Point zero five or five percent will calculate based on that number and then use a goal, seeking to adjust it. So I'm going to say let's say this is the negative or negative present value shift nine, the rate five percent that we're guessing right now, comma number of periods is going to be then twenty five comma. The payment is still going to be the 90 and enter that will see the present value of this one thousand negative present value shift nine rate is going to be, we're guessing that five percent comma number of periods.

Twenty five comma comma because not an annuity. We're going to then pick up the future value of one thousand. If we present the value of those two, adding these two up we would get two one five six three seven six. We want to get two one one one five so we can adjust it by changing this number to get closer and closer and use goals. Seek to simply do that for us. So let's use the Google Data tab up top. We're going to go to the what if analysis in the forecast chapter. Go see what's the goal that you seek, says Excel. We have a noble goal of seeking that. This will be this number one one one five by changing by changing this cell, could you help us seek that goal? And we'll say, OK, and it feels like, yeah, it comes out to seven point nine three. Goal has been sought, goal has been found.

So, Of course, that rate is lower than the nine percent as expected. Let's go ahead and do it here with a rate function. This time, the rate function equals the rate shift nine. We have the number of periods, which is going to be the twenty five comma. The payment is going to be ninety comma. The present value we're going to say is the one one one five comma. Future value is going to be one thousand. However, we know that the future value needs to be negative and the payment over here needs to have negative results. The function doesn't work right and it's annoying. So we're going negative there. So there we have it. Now, this matches this up here.

This is the easier way to do it. But even if done that way, I would double check it by doing your calculation. Annuity present value of one calculation. Once we have that market rate now, we can do our same calculation to then think about, well, what's the cost after tax? That's basically the cost before tax. What's going to be the cost after tax? So we're in a similar situation, just making sure that we're picking up the right number to be using here. We're going to take the interest rate market, by the way, market rate, which is going to be what we just calculated, the seven point nine three percent to find it home tab numbers group percent to five, add in a couple decimals. Then we're going to be picking up the one minus the tax rate and Colen and we'll have one. And then the tax rate, which is going to be here, which is going to be the thirty five percent, let's make those two percent to five numbers percent to fire them.

Underline the thirty five part group and underline this is going to be a Subbuteo total and then we'll take the one hundred percent minus the thirty five percent percent to find that number, a group percent divide. And then we're going to indent these two for the fun of it alignment and dent. It's not just fun, it looks better. Subtotal alignment and dent. And then we're going to call this the cost of debt after tax, which is going to be the seven point nine, three times the sixty five percent percent to find it numbers percent to five. Add in a couple of decimals and underline in here font group and underline. So there we have it now it's kind of proof of our calculation by doing it with, with our example over here. Kind of a longer calculation, but I think it's one that ties it together a little bit easier.

So we got the interest component. What's the interest calculation? Normally it would be the debt, which would be the face amount of the one thousand, and then we would multiply that times the interest rate, which this time is the market rate. This is the confusing component because you're not paying based on the market rate, but due to the fact that you had to issue it in this case at a premium, you will be amortizing that premium and basically hopefully expensing it, hopefully it being deductible and whatnot. And therefore that's why you use the market rate. So we're saying market rate then at the nine point or seven point nine three, as opposed to the nine percent, which would be ninety divided by one thousand or the rate on the bond, that's going to be the interest in.

Arrest, and that's going to be equal to the one thousand times that market rate, add in a couple of decimals, numbers, decimals, and then let's indent these, go into the alignment and dent and dent this one again, alignment and indent. Then we're going to go to the tax benefit. What's the tax benefit then of this? Well, we'll tell you it's the interest expense expense deduction that you would get on average over the life of this thing, which would be the seventy nine, twenty nine, adding some decimals, no group decimals, and then multiply times the tax rate, which I'll just say equals the tax rate over here, which is that 35 percent and making that eight percent numbers group percent defined it, fought group underlining it and then multiplying that out seventy nine point two nine times to thirty five percent, adding pennies numbers drop a couple of pennies.

That's going to be the tax benefit. All right, then we'll go ahead and indent these two or three alignment and dent. Alignment and again, so then we can subtract those two out and give us the cost of debt after taxes on a dollar basis, which would be the seventy nine point two nine minus the twenty seven seventy five adding decimals numbers group, a couple of decimals, underlining the twenty seven font group underline. And then we could think about, well what about on a percentage basis if I took the cost of debt after tax per percent is what we want now we could say, all right, well then we'll just take the cost of debt after taxes here, which we just calculated on a dollar basis, adding decimals, no group decimals.

Compare it to the debt itself, which was the one thousand face amount of the bond that we had to pay at maturity. And that's going to give us the cost of debt. After-Tax per cent. And we'll just divide that out then. So that's what we'll do. The fifty one fifty four divided by the one thousand and then we're going to go to the No group. Make that a percent. And there we have it, let's do some indentations here, alignment and dent down here, alignment and dent and and there we have it at the five point one five.

Calculate Change in Cost of Debt After Tax Due to Reduced Tax

We're going to say that the tax rate has changed from thirty five to twenty five. Consider that that will have an impact then on the market rate or the yield to maturity and then do a recalculation for similar bonds that could be issued at that point in time in the future. So our original data up top, we've got the bond outstanding. We're going to say the rate on the bond is going to be nine percent. The yield to maturity is going to be the 12 percent, basically the market rate here and then the tax rate is going to be then the thirty five percent. So we'll calculate our after tax basically impact in a similar fashion as we would with other types of debt.

Noting that the confusing thing here is that we have to basically rate what we're using. Which rate do we use? We're going to be paying interest based on the nine percent. However, the market rate is really going to drive ultimately what we have with the interest, because we'll have to amortize basically the premium or discount and that's basically interest. So we are going to use the market rate or yield to maturity. That's what can be kind of confusing about the bonds. Also note that in a prior chapter, we were not given this rate, but rather the price and have to solve for that rate. And that added a level of complexity. Now we're given the rate here.

We just need to make sure that we pick the proper rate in order to do the calculation than do our standard calculation, which will be the interest rate. So the interest rate, which I'm going to say is the market rate and we're going to be picking up, then the 12 percent make that eight percent by going into the numbers per cent to find it. Then we have the one minus the tax rate brackets, coal, and we'll pick up the one. Tax rate is going to be the thirty five percent, the thirty five percent on the tax rate, let's make that a percent. Let's make both of these percentages go into the No group percent to find it.

Underlining the second one font group and underline this will be a subtotal we'll call it, bringing this into the our column, which will be the one hundred percent minus the thirty five percent making that eight percent number of group percent to five. And then fourth group underline then we have let's do some indentations here, alignment and dent subtotal. And then finally we have the cost of debt after tax. And wanted to add a little suspense here on that before we got to the answer. So 12 percent times the sixty five percent that then if we go to the No group, percent to add some decimals, we're at the seven point eight. So if we do that in our example up top, just to basically verify our numbers over here, we can then think, OK, let's do the recalculation.

As you might basically think of the calculation from top to bottom, calculating the interest first and we'd say the interest calculation would typically be then the debt. Which I'm going to assume is going to be the one thousand down here, notice we didn't even really need the debt in order to calculate the cost, but it's often useful to think about the debt. Plug in a number. If you don't have one to mull this over in your mind, then we're looking at the interest rate and this is going to be the market. Once again, you're going to say, well, I'm not actually paying interest on the market rate. I'm paying interest on the rate on the bond. Why am I using the market rate? Because the difference between the do the the discount or premium would have to then be reconciled between the difference in the purchase price in the face and about the bond. And that would basically be the interest.

So you could use different methods to do that. From an accounting standpoint, possibly. But that's kind of the reason. That's what the confusing kind of component is here. So we're thinking kind of like an average for a year to year component. We're not using the bond rate, but the yield to maturity or market rate. So then we're going to say, all right, that means that the interest. Because then on average is going to be the one thousand times that 12 percent will pick up that 12 percent, we don't really need the decimal. I'll take the decimals off this time to take the decimals off, and then that'll be our interest. Let's do some indentations by going to the alignment and dent.

That's going to be our interest. And then we can think about, OK, well, what would the tax benefit then be able to say? Tax benefit on average, then being the interest, which is going to be the interest. The Dukan in this case deduct John for taxes, which we're going to say is that one twenty. So we'll pick up the one 20 times the tax rate, which is going to be that. Thirty five percent. The tax rate is thirty five. Let's pick it up over here, making that eight percent number, making it eight percent. That's going to give us the tax benefit put in this in the outer column. This is going to be the one twenty times to the thirty five percent for the tax benefit. Let's add a couple of decimals numbers group, a couple of decimals there, underline on the thirty five with the font and underline let's indent selecting these three cells alignment and dent this one here alignment indent again.

So then that'll give us the cost on a dollar basis. Cost of debt after taxes of the one twenty minus the forty two and let's go ahead and we don't really need the decimals up top here and let's just get rid of the decimals, don't need them. And then I'll underline here so will underline there and then we want to see that on a percentage basis. So cost of debt after tax per cent and then Cohon would be the cost of debt after taxes that we got over here, the seventy eight, comparing it to the debt itself, which we assumed here to be the one thousand. So the one thousand underlining font group and underline that'll be then the cost of debt after taxes there. I'm sorry. That's going to be. The cost of debt after taxes percent. There we go.

That's what we wanted and that's going to be the seventy eight divided by the one thousand. Add in a couple decimals and percent to find numbers percent. If I add a couple of decimals, there's the 787. Eighty 80. Let's do some indentations here. Selecting these three alignment and dent all indent this one again. OK, so then we're going to assume that some changes happen, there's a change to the law, let's say the tax rate goes down to twenty five percent and that has an impact on the market. So the tax rate change results in a yield to maturity change to 10 percent. So what would be the cost of the debt if we were to issue kind of similar debt at this point in time on a percentage basis where we've got to where was if we wanted to get we've got to recalculate this thing then and we'll say, all right, this is going to be the interest rate, interest rate and we're going to use the market rate again.

This time, the market rate that they gave us was the 10 percent rate, that 10 percent this time. That's what that's what it says. That's what it says. That's what I'm using, 10 percent. And then we have the brackets, one minus the tax rate shift zero Kolan. And then we have one tax rate that is going to be this tax rate change. Keep that. That's going to be equal to the twenty five percent making those two percent by go into the No group percent fine under the twenty five percent will go to the fort and underline their let's call this a subtotal because it's under the bottom, it's underneath, it's going to be the one hundred minus to twenty five and making that eight percent number numbers percent defined.

Let's underline Phonte underline and then let's do some indentations. Adding suspense to the bottom line number here. Alignment and dent subtotal and dent. And then finally the bottom line number called cost of debt after tax will be 10 percent times the 75 percent making it a percent, no group percent to find. Add in a couple of decimals. Now we're looking at seven point five as opposed to the seven point eight before. If we just kind of recalculate it in our example over here, which I think is the most straightforward way to kind of think about this, which there the interest then on average would be if we had the debt. Let's just say the debt was that thousand dollars. We're assuming a thousand dollars on the bond.

And then the rate that we're going to use, the interest rate, interest rate and we're going to use the market rate, given the reasons we had before, even though we're going to be paying based on the the rate on the bond, when you take into account the the discount or premium that has to be amortized, then on average we're actually using the market rate here. That's kind of confusing. So we're going to be picking up then the 10 percent over here, the 10 percent, and then that's going to be the interest we'll calculate at the one thousand times the 10 percent market rate interest basically on average over the life of the bond here. Let's highlight these three or select them and then alignment and dent interest, alignment and debt again.

And then the question, Of course, is, Will, what's the tax benefit tax benefit on average, yearly on average? Basically, it's going to be the interest deduction that we have and that's going to be the one thousand now, the one thousand interest deduction times the tax rate, which is going to be the tax rate, which we said was at twenty five percent. Twenty five percent on the tax rate numbers group, percent to find it for that group underlining it. That's going to be the tax benefit on the outside here. That's going to be one hundred times the twenty five percent or twenty five. Let's do some indentation selecting these items, alignment and dent going to indent the tax benefit again, alignment.

And again, let's put an underline here and underline that's going to give us the cost of debt after tax on a dollar basis, which would be the one thousand minus the twenty five. And then we'd have to say what I want to see the cost of debt after tax on a percentage basis. So it will be like, all right, that's not a problem. We'll take the cost of debt after tax seventy five and we'll compare that to the debt itself. Up top face amount of the bond, which was one thousand, put an underlying there fought group underline. And that's going to give us the cost of debt after tax per cent on the outside here, comparing the seventy five divided by the one thousand making that a percent, no group percent to find it, adding a couple of decimals. We get back to that seven point five, seven point five. Let's do some indenting selecting these guys, these items, these columns, these cells, alignment indent and then the cost of the debt alignment.

Cost of Preferred Stock Percent

We're thinking about the debt financing, which we looked at in the past, this time we're looking at the equity financing, starting with the preferred stock, and then we'll move onto the common stock, the preferred stock on the equity side of things, typically being a little bit easier due to the restrictive nature of the preferred stock. It's also a little bit easier in some cases than the debt financing due to the fact that when we think about debt financing, we have to deal, Of course, with the interest, which is going to be the cost that will be there for the debt financing. With regards to the preferred stock, the cost that we're talking about would be the dividends typically that would be paying out our major cost. And on the debt financing, the interest that we have to pay actually has a tax consequence.

As we saw in that, you could have a tax benefit of the interest that is being paid. So you've got to take that into consideration. We don't have that same kind of consideration here. Dealing on the equity side of things, therefore, can actually be a little bit more straightforward of a calculation. So we have the preferred stock. We're going to say that we can sell the preferred stock for one hundred and fifty dollars, the estimated flotation costs, the cost of us basically issuing the preferred stock. Basically, the administration cost of us issuing the stock would be four dollars. And then we're going to have the major cost to us, which means the dividends we the company paying out dividends to the preferred stockholders, which are going to be nine dollars on an annual basis.

So we're kind of calculating this basically on an annual basis here. So we're going to separate what's the cost of preferred stock on percent we can take then the annual dividends. Let's start with the annual dividends. That's basically the major cost that we have, which is going to be the nine dollars. We're saying it's nine dollars. And then I'm going to say the net sales price. Let's call this because I'm going to subtract out what we're going to get, the 150 minus the cost of us getting it, the four dollars. Let's take the 150 sales price, let's call it let's call it the sales price of preferred stock. And that's going to be then the one fifty minus the estimated flotation cost, which we're going to say is four dollars, which will give us the net sales price.

And I'll pull that to the outside here, which is the one fifty minus the four. So basically after those flotation costs, we're going to get the one forty six. I'm going to go to the home tab then Phonte Group and underline going to select these items and an indent them, go into the alignment group and indent then the net sales alignment group. And again that's going to give us then the cost of preferred stock per cent that we'll have and that's going to be equal to the cost, the dividends that we're going to be paying out on an annual basis. We're assuming here, divided by the one forty six cost and that's going to give us our percent number of group percent to find it. We can then add a couple of decimals.

We're looking about six point one six percent going to go ahead and underline here home tab font and underline. So note again, a little bit more simplified because Of course we're not dealing with the interest. The cost is going to be the dividends that we have up top end because this is going to be equity coming out of the equity. We don't have something resulting on the income statement with this transaction and therefore it shouldn't have an impact on the taxes as well. So we don't have that kind of tax impact. We're comparing the annual dividends that we have, which should be somewhat standardized for the preferred stock to then the net price, meaning the one fifty minus the cost of us issuing one fifty. We received minus the cost of issuing giving us that six point one six percent in this case.

Calculate Preferred Stock Current Yield

We're looking here on the equity side of things and therefore not having to worry so much about the tax impact, given the fact that we have equity financing as opposed to debt, which includes interest, typically something that will be deductible and therefore has a tax impact. So preferred stock. We have preferred stock issued in the past. We're going to imagine this stock was issued at two hundred. Our value, the yield at the time of issuance is 10 percent. We're saying the current price is now one seventy five. So we want to figure out what the current yield is at this point in time.

So we're going to that. All right. Let's go ahead and pick up the I'm going to calculate the annual dividend dividend payment payment because they didn't give us the payment. They gave us basically the things that we need to calculate it, that being the two hundred and ten percent here. So I'm going to say the par value is going to be equal to two hundred dollars. And then we have the yield at time of issuance, we'll call it. That was the 10 percent. So picking up the 10 percent, let's put a percent thereby go into the No group percent to find it font group and underline it. That will then give us our annual dividend dividend payment which is going to be in our column. I'm going to be picking up two hundred times the 10 percent. That's going to be twenty dollars.

And let's go ahead and add some formatting here by going to the alignment, increase the indenting, I'm going to increase the indenting again. So there we have that. And then this is going to be the the current let's call the current market market price that we're going to be comparing to that being then now at the one seventy five, going to put an underline here for that group and underline and that'll give us our current yield, which would then be equal to the twenty dollars of the dividend divided by the price of one seventy five. And then if we go to the numbers group and percentage by that we're looking at eleven, let's add a couple of decimals, eleven point four, three percent. So nope, we kind of this is kind of a reverse or backing into a way for the current yield here.

So we had to figure this out in order to figure this out, we had to figure out the dividend, which is simply going to be what it was issued for the times, the yield at the time of issuance. That'll give us our twenty dollars. That would be our dividend. That often is something that we might know basically in practice. We're going to compare that then to the current market price, which in this case it's going to be one seventy five. So that twenty divided by the one seventy five gives us our current yield that compares the dividend to the current market price of eleven point four three percent.

Financing Debt vs Preferred Stock

We're thinking about debt, we have to add on the added complexity of the tax impact of it. So we have the debt. We're saying the can issue at yield to maturity of the 12 percent. So this is now giving us yield to maturity. We're thinking of a possible bond here, but all we really need is the rate and not all the information on the bond due to the fact that they gave us, in essence, the market rate, the yield to maturity rate, not the rate on the bond. That's the one that we can use with our normal kind of debt type of calculation to then take into consideration the impact of the tax. So note, what we're not doing is actually adding or putting in place a dollar amount here. We're doing this just with the basic percents, again, doing our comparison between the debt financing and the equity in this case, the preferred stock tax rate, then.

Thirty five percent. We have then the preferred stock down below with the price at the seventy five, the floating cost, the cost issue, the preferred stock. In other words, the 10 and the annual dividend we're going to say is the six dollars on the dividend down here in the preferred stock side of things, we've got the dividends that we'll have to take into consideration, but we don't have that tax impact. So those are going to be some of the differences here. So then we're going to go do our calculations. So let's do our cost of debt after tax. We're going to say that the interest rate, let's say the interest rate is going to be then the 12 percent on it. That would be the normal cost. But we have to then take into consideration the tax impact so we can compare it to the equity, which doesn't have a tax impact comparison.

As they say, apples to apples, numbers group percent define it or the same thing to the same thing. That's what it means, apples to apples. So one minus the tax rate shift zero Colen. And this is going to be the one and then we'll pick up the tax rate, the rate of the tax, which is going to be equal to that. Thirty five percent make that eight percent by going into the numbers group. Percent define it. Go into the fourth group then and underlining it, we could then make this one over here a percent as well. It might be useful now. It's one hundred percent, one minus the tax rate, one minus point thirty five or one hundred percent, minus thirty five percent.

Same thing. And then we can say the subtotal subtotal is going to then be equal to the one hundred percent minus the thirty five percent making that a percent numbers group percent define it and underline the group. Underline that then let's do some indentations here, alignment and dent in Dent this one again because that's what, that looks good that way. So the cost of debt after tax is going to be twelve times the sixty five. Let's make that a percent numbers group percent add a couple decimals. So there we've got the seven point eight percent that we could think about this as just basically plugging in a number just to see what the impact would be.

And let's say let's say we calculate this out and say, let's say Intourist. Cohen, and let's say that we have the debt and let's just use the amount of the preferred stock. Price here for one preferred stock, so let's just use that for our comparison, if we have the debt for that and then the interest rate is going to be for the debt this time on the debt side of things, is that 12 percent. So then we could say that the interest expense, expense on average then is going to be equal to seventy five times the 12 going to go ahead and add some decimals there. No group, add a couple of decimals, going to select these three items and then go to the alignment and dent it and then indent this one again. And then we're going to see the tax impact, we the tax impact because we're looking at the debit side of things. Tax benefits are good.

So then we're going to pick up the interest, which is now an interest deduction, which would be that nine dollars, because we get the benefit of the taxes on that. The tax rate times, the tax rate, which I'll just pick up right here, is the thirty five percent you'll recall, because that's what we read on the left, no group percentage high. And then Ford Group and underline. And that's going to give us our tax benefit, which is misspelled up top, which normally doesn't bother me, but that's bothering me right now. So I'm going to change it. There we go. And then this is going to be then the nine times the thirty five percent. Let's add some decimals here by going into the no group, add a couple of decimals, do some indentations selecting these three sales, go into the alignment indent and then selecting this one alignment indent again.

That looks nicer. Now we want to think about the cost of debt after taxes, which will be equal to the nine dollars minus the three point one five, adding some decimals. Their numbers group decimals put in an underline under the three point one five. So there we have that now if we want that's in terms of a dollar amount. Then if we add then the percent, what would the percent then be? Cost of debt after tax percent coal and would be equal to the cost of debt in terms of a dollar basis, that five point eighty five. And let's add some decimal numbers just to normalize and we'll compare that to the debt itself. That's going to be equal to the seventy five what we started with, and that'll give us the cost of debt after tax.

And we'll say that that's going to be equal to the five point eight five divided by the seventy five, making that a percent numbers group percentage by adding a couple of decimals, underlining here for each group and underline. So we get back to that seven point eight. It's kind of verifying what we did over here on a percentage basis. Now let's think about the preferred stock going down to the preferred stock, what's happening in the preferred stock world. If we did this that way on the equity side of things, well, the price is going to be seventy five. We're going to say that the floating cost, the cost issue, the preferred stock, in other words, ten and the annual dividend, what we have to pay then on an annual basis, six.

So we're going to say, OK, well let's take the annual let's take the annual dividend here. We'll pick up the total annual dividend and this is going to be equal to six. Put this in your column and then I'm going to pick up what I'm going to call the net sales price. So net sales Colen, which is going to be the price. So the sales price here at the seventy five mine is the floating cost because we had to pay those in order to issue this stock. So that's going to be the ten dollars that it cost us to do that, which seems kind of high. And then we're going to say that's going to be the net sales which will be equal to seventy five minus the ten. So we got sixty five. Let's do some formatting here. Selecting these three cells alignment and selecting this one alignment indent looks way nicer that way.

And then under the ten we're going to go to the front group and then underline and then we're going to finally get to the cost of preferred stock percent, which will be equal to the six divided by sixty five. Much more straightforward type of calculation here. Not having to deal with taxes, you'll, you'll note. So we have the number and let's go ahead and percent defy that. That's going to be nine. Let's add a couple of decimals because it's really nine points to three about. So the difference between the two is the difference between the options. Difference between the options is going to be equal to the seven point eight minus the nine point two three. So it looks like the lesser amount of the cost of debt after tax would be the seven point eight on the debt side of things.

The difference being the one point four, six percent going to put it under line here as well. Phonte Group. And then underline note that you can't kind of think this through a little bit in more detail. If we think about the debt up top, the seventy five dollars we're seeing to get the seventy five dollars it's going to cost us, we're saying on average yearly the nine dollars, that nine dollars is something that's going to continue for the life of whatever the debt is in this case, if it a bond or something like that, if it's a 30 year bond, we're thinking for 30 years we would have that and then we'd have basically the cost of the bond that it but it would end or mature at some point in time.

Then we have the tax benefit, which once again is something that we would expect basically on average annually. Therefore, the costs we're seeing here at the five point eight five is basically the net cost kind of on an annual basis for the life of the bond to receive that. Seventy five down here. It's a little bit different down here. Note that we have the seventy five dollars, but we're not really receiving the seventy five or subtracting out the flotation costs first. That caused us to question its meaning. When we first basically set this up, we're not actually getting the seventy five, we're getting the sixty five because these costs are not annual costs are not, things are going to be repetitive.

There are things that are going to be there for the issuance. If we're one of the 75 that I'd have to up this in some way to get it to eighty five or something in order to account for the flotation cost. So that's one thing to keep in mind. And the other thing that's to keep in mind here, Of course, is the annual dividends are something that here are going to be basically annual. There's no end date, there's no set maturity date as well. So that's another thing to basically just understand when you think about the comparisons between these items. But this will give you basically an idea and the percentage will give you something, Of course, that'll give you the comparability between the options.

Financing Common Stock Prob 1

We think about financing the company, we have the two broad categories we've looked at in prior chapters, the debt side of things when thinking about the debt side of financing to pull in money for the company, we have to take into consideration the tax impact due to the fact that the cost of debt is usually paid like rent interest, usually deductible. That's an income statement item. Therefore, tax impact because we're talking income tax impact. When we look at the equity side of things we usually have, the common stock is what we're thinking of, although we could issue the preferred stock as well. We looked at the preferred stock in prior chapters because it's a little bit easier due to the constraints of the preferred stock.

Now we're moving to the common stock, which is a little bit more complex because there's multiple components of the common stock. So now we're talking about the issuance of the common stock in order to finance the company. Note when we're talking about the cost of the common stock, we're not talking about normal trading that happens on like the stock market. When you hear about stocks being traded, note that that's usually, Of course, being traded from stocks that have already been issued from the company and now are being traded amongst the others on the stock market here. We're talking about the issuance of new shares in the company. So new shares are going from the company. Therefore, when someone buys these shares, the money's going directly to the company, financing the company.

Now, obviously, when that happens, we're issuing stocks which are considered like the ownership portion of the company. So we have to, one, be considering, you know, what the impact is in terms of the ownership, the voting rights and whatnot that could be out there with regards to the issuance of the stock, then we also want to issue just a cash flow. What's going to be the cash flow kind of impact in terms of the issuance of the stock and what's going to be the cost in terms of the issuance of the stock with regards to both cash flow, which would be the dividends that we're going to be issuing as well as the value of the stock? Because what what has been given up, Of course, is is the equity interest in the stock and the value as the value of the stock goes up, that equity interest could be paid out in the in the form of dividends, or it could be basically in the growth of the company, which would increase basically the value of the stocks that the owners have.

So those are the two things that we have to kind of keep in mind when we're thinking about the cost. So we have the information and the dividends are something that we get. We're going to have to assume that we're going to be paying we're going to say on an annual basis at this point, the two dollars on the dividends, dividends and common stock, like with the preferred stock, but different than the bonds are something that, Of course, there's no real end date on. We can think of them going out for a long time, whereas there's a maturity date when we think about interest payments on, say, something like a bond. So that's something just to keep in mind. We have the common stock price. This is what we think we can offer them for.

So that's how much we're going to be receiving per stock, in essence. And then we have the expected growth. That's going to be the twelve percent. When we give the common stock that now has an equity interest in the organization, they're going to get the dividends. But they also get the increase in basically the value because they're kind of like owners of the organization. So if you think about assets minus liabilities equals the equity interest they have kind of like an interest in the equity interest. As the equity goes up, then they have that equity interest as well. That also can be considered kind of a cost there, although you can kind of separate a cash flow situation versus the increase in value depending on what your particular needs are.

So we're looking at the cost then of the retained earnings and then we can also add in the flotation cost. So we'll do it first without the flotation costs, which would be the cost of us to issue the common stock. And then we'll add the flotation cost to the flotation cost. Hopefully usually would be something that's kind of like in material, given the amount that that's going to be issued, but maybe something that we want to take into consideration when doing comparisons. OK, so we want to look at this on a percentage basis. That's something that we can basically compare and contrast to some of our other options, such as the debt options. So to do that, let's say that we have the dividends per share. That's something that we're going to have to pay out. That's going to be a cost. So I'll pick up the dividends per share, which is going to be the two dollars.

We're going to be comparing that then to the common stock price. The common stock price, we're going to say, is forty dollars. So the forty dollars in this case is the price. But that's what we expect to receive because. We're the ones selling it. So in order to receive the common stock price, in this case 40 per share, then it's going to cost us two dollars in dividends, basically on an annual basis. So if we divide that out, we're going to have a subtotal, we'll call it subtotal, and that's going to be equal to the two divided by the 40 making that then eight percent and the No group percent to find it. I'm going to go ahead and indent this tab as well. Alignment and indent.

So there's the five percent and then we're going to add to that. So that would be basically the cost of it, kind of like a cash flow basis. But then we got to add to that the expected growth, because the expected growth is something that is also going to be included in the cost. That's what we're giving up to some degree here. So we're also going to say the expected growth is going to be 12 percent. So it's going to grow by 12 percent. And we're going to see that annual growth here. So we'll just say no group percent to FI. And we're going to add then the expected growth to get to the cost of retained earnings. And I'm going to say this is going to be then equal to the five plus the 12 five plus the 12 numbers group and percent to five that's going to be our 17.

Let's underline the 12 font group and underline. And so there we have that. We're looking at 17 percent. So here's the formula. And we could make a distinction of the cost of retained earnings, which which we're just going to say doesn't include the flotation costs versus the cost of common stock, which means we're going to include the flotation costs, the formula dividends divided by the common stock price, plus the growth rate. So pretty straightforward, but be careful with the formula here that it's not dividends divided by a common stock price. In other words, there's no quotation marks around here. Therefore, we do the division first order of operations, then we add the growth rate.

So now let's say, well, what if we add in the cost of the flotation costs down here? And so we'll tack on the flotation costs formula that is just going to be slightly different. We're going to say the common stock, the cost of the common stock is going to be the dividends divided by now. We've got the brackets, common stock price minus the flotation costs, and then we will add the growth rate. So it'll be slightly different, same kind of process. So we're going to say the dividend, same same point here will say dividends per share. We're going to say two dollars. I'm going to put this into the middle column this time and add one little subcategory to kind of pull this out in our table. And that's going to be the net price. So net price, Colen.

And this is where we do our little flotation cost, which is going to be the common stock price, the price of the common stock, which we're going to say is equal to you. I'm going to put this in the inner column, the forty dollars, but then there's the cost of the flotation cost. So we've got to subtract that out. That's the cost of us to issue, in essence, the stock, which we're going to say is four dollars. That's our kind of one time cost rather than a cost that's going to be recurring. And therefore we're going to calculate the net amount that we would then be getting to issue the stock. So we're going to go and underline, and that's going to give us basically our net price, we'll call it, which is going to be equal to forty minus the four. So we're really going to get thirty six after this kind of one time cost.

Selecting these three cells alignment indent, we're going to indent the net price again and denim that is going to underline the thirty six. So we're going to go to the group and underline now we're to the same point that basically we have up top instead of having the forty we're basically taking the net, which is the thirty six after the flotation cost, then we're going to add the cost of make this are subtotal subtotal which is then going to be equal to the two divided by the thirty six. I'm going to increase the percentage by that. We're going to say let's go to the numbers percent. If five add a couple of decimals, five point five six and then we're simply going to add to that our growth rate. So we're going to say the growth rate will be here. And also note the difference here between this cost, that being kind of our net price because it's one time versus the dividends, which is an annual cost. So let's keep that in mind.

And then the expected growth, which we're saying is annual, is going to be that 12 percent, 12 percent percent to find the cell numbers group percent to five underlying font group and then underline and that'll give us our end result, which is the cost of common stock we're going to call it. And that will be equal. Use the trustees some function this time because that's good to use some in those up or adding them up. And then we'll add the good old percent numbers percent. If I add a couple of decimals, we're looking at seventeen point five, six versus the seventeen. If we take into consideration the flotation costs, the cost of us to issue the one time cost of the issuing of the stock.

What Next

Now looking at the common stock issuance for the equity financing as opposed to the preferred stock, the common stock, probably the most common thing we would think of with equity financing. Remember, we're talking about or thinking of the issuance of the stock from the organization when stocks trade on the exchange. Usually it's being traded amongst stocks that have been already issued. We're talking about here the company issuing the stock, the money, then going to the organization in order to finance the operations when stock is issued. We then have value that's going out there.

Having the owner or an ownership interest is basically thought of to be being sold. So in essence, we can think about the cost as basically kind of the net value of the organization from a bookkeeping standpoint, assets minus liabilities or basically the retained earnings. We can think about that from the standpoint of dividends that will be paid in the future, our commitments to dividends. And we can also try to think about that in terms of the estimated growth in the value of the organization that is now a piece of it being owned. Now, when we issue the equity interest. OK, so let's go through our calculation here. We're going to do this two different ways.

We're going to add the flotation costs in the second one, and we'll call that the cost of common stock versus the cost of retained earnings, retained earnings. As you know, the accounting equation would be, you know, if you take assets minus liabilities, you've got the retained earnings, which you can think of kind of like the value of the organization in that format. So when we issue common stock to owners, they own the company and therefore they have a claim to what you would think about as kind of like the equity chapter of the organization. That's one way to kind of mull it over. So we'll have the dividends, let's calculate the dividends here. We're going to estimate that the dividends are going to be paid per share.

That could go basically indefinitely because the dividends will be paid out. There's no maturity date per say. I'm going to put that in the inner column here. It's going to be four dollars and we're going to then take the common stock price, common stock price. This is what we're going to receive, the ninety dollars per share issued because that's what we can sell it for on the market. Ford Group underline. And then we've got the subtotal. I'm just going to call it subtotals, the total below the calculation, which is going to be the four dollars divided by the 90 subtotal being the if we add the percent numbers group percent. If I add a couple of decimals, I'm going to indent then the subtotal alignment group and dent four point four for now.

Then we're going to add to that. We could think about that. It's kind of like the cash flow situation of it. But then we also have the value of the common stock, which I'm going to add to it as well. So that's going to be the growth of the stock because that's also something that is basically in the cost here. And that's going to be then we're going to say it's growing by six percent. That, Of course, would have to be estimated to some degree. We have the numbers group. We've got the percent we're going to underline in the Ford group and underline. That'll give us a total we're going to call cost of retained earnings of and we're going to just add these two up the four point four four plus the six adding or making that eight percent numbers group percent and then add a couple of decimals.

We're looking ten point four for about here's the calculation for it down below cost of retained earnings equaling the dividends divided by the common stock price. Remember, you do this first and then add the growth rate. Now, if we add on the flotation costs, we're going to call that the cost of common stock, basically the same thing. But now we're going to take into consideration the fact that in order to issue the 90 dollar price, it's going to cost us, we're going to say three dollars basically, and just one time fees to get it done to get that done.

So now we'll add one level of complication calculation looking like this common stock or they cost the common stock basically kind of same thing here, except it was taken into consideration that one added one time cost, which is the dividends divided by the common stock price, minus the flotation cost, which you can think of as like the net sales price for the stock plus the growth rate. So the same kind of thing. One more sub calculation. Let's take a look at it and say, well, what if the dividends are still dividends, are still the four dollars? I'm going to put that into our middle column here, middle column. Then I'm going to count the net price. We're looking for the net price now. So I'm going to say net price, and that's going to be the common stock price.

Common stock. Which I'm going to say is equal to the ninety dollars minus what it cost for us to issue it, which we're going to call the flotation costs, because I'm not sure why they call them flotation, cos to be honest, they're floating cost, but those are the one time fees and whatnot to float the stocks out into the marketplace where they can be grabbed for ninety dollars. So we're going to then say, let's go to the Ford Group and underline and subtract those out and that's going to give us the net price. So the net price then equals ninety minus the three.

So now we're going to get the eighty seven after that one time floating cost and then we're going to go to the font group and underline that and let's do some indentations here, go into the alignment and dent net price, let's indent alignment and dent that again looks way nicer that way than subtotal subtotal. We're then going to say this is going to be equal to the four divided by the eighty seven. Let's go ahead and add percent to five. No group percent couple decimals. We're looking at about four point six percent. Then we're going to add the growth that needs to be added. So now we're just going to add the growth again. At this point, we're right to basically the same kind of area we did up top. The only difference is that now we have that subtotal after the one time cost.

So then we're going to add the growth, which is going to be the six percent making that eight percent number of group percent define it. Let's underline Ford Group and underline that's going to give us our cost of common stock. I'm going to use the trustees some function to add them up this time. some of those to add in those two numbers up, making it a percent, no group percent to five, a couple of decimals. We got the ten point six percent. Let's do it again. New set of problems. We're going to do this a few times. I'll go through it a bit more quickly here.

Retained earnings. We got the dividends per share of the one point to this time. So that's how much it's going to cost us on an annual basis. Common stock price is fifty one.

So when we issue the shares, we're getting fifty one dollars per share. That's the market price. That's what we can get for them. We're going to get whatever we can. We are issuing them to the market here. The expected growth rate is going to be eleven percent. So that's also part of the value that will be given, flotation costs four dollars. So let's calculate this, which we'll call the cost of retained earnings, basically the cost before considering the flotation cost here. So we're going to write. Then the dividends are going to be here and we'll calculate the dividends at the one point two, one point two on the dividend. And let's add a decimal so we can see the twenty cents numbers group. There's twenty cents right there.

And then we're going to go to the common stock price, comparing that then to the common stock price. So it's going to cost us one one dollar and twenty six twenty cents to get fifty one dollars per share. Underlining that group and underline that's going to give us our subtotal subtotal and that's going to be equal to the one point to one dollar, twenty cents divided by the fifty one sales price, making that into a percent no group percentage by adding a couple of decimals for it. Let's go ahead and indent the subtotal. Then we're simply going to tack on to that, adding on the expected growth rate, because that's what we're giving up to, because we're giving up.

Basically, you can think of it as a component of retained earnings of assets minus liabilities of the net assets. You can think of it. And those net assets, we expect to grow by 11 percent. So 11 percent. So no group percent to find the eleven underlying fine groups and underline. And that will then give us the cost of retained earnings, some function. TRUSTe, um, of those two items will then percent to five. That number of groups percent to five adds a couple of decimals. We're looking at thirteen points three five. Let's add the flotation cost and call it a whole new thing. Call it the cost of common stock. Basically the same thing here. But now add in the four dollars for the flotation, meaning we're not really getting the fifty one. We have that one time cost.

Fifty one minus four is kind of what we're getting. So let's just add that into our calculations so we'll see. No problem. We got the dividends, dividends. I'm going to put that into the middle column this time, making it a three column worksheet, more advanced three column worksheet, and then we're going to go to the numbers group and add a couple of decimals. There's the one twenty and then we're going to calculate the net price instead of just the price, because we've got to add the nuance of the flotation cost because they can be kind of expensive, actually, those flotation costs. And that's going to be equal to fifty one fifty one. And then we've got the flotation costs, which is the one.

Time, cost of issuing these things is going to be four dollars, and let's underline that we're going to say the fighting group and then underline that it's going to give us our net prize. So I call it the net price because that's what it's called and that I misspelled it up here. So I'm going to fix it. That might be bothering people. And then I'll subtract this out. Fifty one minus the four that's going to give us our forty seven on the net price. Let's underline that font group. Now we're going to compare the dividends not to the price but the net price. But before we do, let's do some indentation selecting these three cells, alignment and dent and then the net price and the intent that again that looks way better.

Then we have the subtotal outer column this time comparing the one 20 dividends we're going to have to pay for the net price, the seventy five that we're going to get after the flotation costs. And then let's add a percent there, no percent a couple of decimals on that one. And then we have to add to that the expected growth rate just like before. Which is 11, so I'm going to say 11 percent. That's what I'm going to say. And then 42 percent Phonte Underline and that's going to be the cost of common stock. TRUSTe Some function equals Sequim of those two numbers, making them into eight percent. No group percent. Add in a couple of decimals. We're looking at thirteen points five five. Let's do it again.

So now the dividends are going to be annual dividends, two point ten, the common stock price. We could sell these on the market for the twenty nine expected growth, nine percent and then the flotation. So we'll calculate the cost of retained earnings, which we're going to say is the cost basically before the flotation cost. That's what we're going to call it. And we're going to say then the dividends this time that's our annual cost is going to be the two point ten. That's what we got to pay out. We've we've that's what we're thinking. We're going to pay out and we're going to compare that to what we're going to get because we're going to sell these things per share. Twenty nine dollars. Twenty nine dollars.

That's how much the market will pay us. So we're going to go to the font group and underline that when we do that comparison, I'll subtract the total below the other stuff. Subscribe to the others, two point ten divided by twenty nine. Then this is going to be a percent. No group percent. Add a couple decimals. Let's indent the subtotal and denim in the alignment group and then tack on or add to it the expected growth as well. And that's going to be the nine percent nine percent number of group percentage five font groups underline. If we add those two up equals the sum we think the cost then is going to be if we make that into a percent sixteen and then a couple of decimals, twenty four, sixteen point two four, that's going to be the cost of retained earnings.

Now let's tack on the flotation costs and call it the cost of capital. So the same kind of process. We're going to say, all right, we still have the dividends. No change there, no change. Their dividends are the dividends. That's the annual cost of the two point ten, which we're putting in the middle column now, because now I want to do a sub calculation, which is going to be called net price. Net price Colen, which will include the common stock price. And that's going to be equal to twenty nine dollars. But then we had to pay a three dollar one time fee to float these things. We don't want these things sinking. And if you want them to float, not sink, you got to play. I don't know.

That doesn't make it a font group underline and this is going to be the net price. The net price is going to be equal to the twenty nine minus the flotation one time cost to get these things floated out there. Twenty six. Let's put an underlying under the twenty six font group and then underline, then we'll take the trusty sub total subtotal. I need to add some pennies to these two dollars because I can't see the ten cents. I'm going to add a couple of decimals. So it's ten, this is the 210. There's a freeway here called the two divided by twenty six and then no group percent add a couple of decimals. We're at eight point eight. Then we'll just tack on once again the expected growth, this time at the nine percent on the expected growth, adding that making it into a percent, underlining it in the font group.

That then is going to give us the cost of common stock. Some function equals some assumption of those two and then no group percent adds a couple decimals like that, seventeen point zero eight. Let's do some indentation here on these three indents. Those make it look nicer alignment. And then I think it's nicer. You might think you might want no need to. Maybe this doesn't look as nice. You know, it's just my opinion of the indentation. It's not a requirement. In other words, let's do this again. Let's do it. Let's do it again. Can we? Yes, we can. We've got the dividends per share now. Seven dollars, the carbon price. Fifty five. The growth at the seven percent and the flotation now six percent.

All right, let's do it again. So this we got the dividends cost of retained earnings, not including the flotation dividends. That's how much it's going to cost annually. That's the seven dollars we've determined this time. And then the common stock price, that's how much we're going to get per share. Fifty five underlining that font group underline. And that's going to give us a subtotal equal to the seven overall divided by the fifty five needed to make that a percent so we could see what's going on. No group percent. Let's add a couple of deaths. We're looking at twelve point seven three, that's what we're looking at.

That's what we're looking at. And then this is going to equal the expected growth, adding or tacking on, plus expected growth, seven percent making that into a percent, no group percent to five. And then let's underline it while we're here, Phonte Group and underline and that's going to give us the cost of retained earnings equal to some function of those two numbers, then Phonte group percent to five, add a couple of decimals. Now let's tackle the flotation cost. Same thing, but with flotation, flotation added the cost, the one time cost of us issuing these stocks. So we'll add that bit of complexity. We still have the dividends that we're going to be paying on an annual basis, looking at seven percent, we're looking at seven percent there.

Then we're going to take the net price. This is the new thing that's happening. New thing right here. Common stock is going to be thirty five. We saw that before. But then the really new part of the new thing is the flotation costs that are added flotation costs, six percent or six dollars. That's how much it costs to float these things out into the market, apparently. So they don't sink. And that's going to give us the net price, net price equaling the fifty five minus the six. Then let's underline that one Ford group and underline and that'll give us then our subtotal sub total or subtotal. And this will be equal to the seven divided by the forty nine. Now the net kind of price makes that a percent, no group percentage by adding a couple of decimals.

Let's go ahead and do some indentation over here to select in these three sales alignment, dent, net price and dent so much nicer I think. I feel like that's worth doing. So then we have the expected growth, add in the expected growth to it too. That's going to be equal to the seven percent, seven percent added on making that a percent no group percent upside. And we don't need any decimals because it's just seven and then five groups and underlines. And then we'll call this the cost of common stock, because that's what it is. We like to call things by what they actually are. That makes things easier for people to understand. So then we're going to say that this is going to be the number of group percent and then a couple of decimals. So we're looking at twenty one point two nine percent.